Knowledge Management

CHANDOS
KNOWLEDGE MANAGEMENT SERIES

Series Editor: Melinda Taylor
(email: melindataylor@chandospublishing.com)

Chandos' new series of books are aimed at all those individuals interested in knowledge management. They have been specially commissioned to provide the reader with an authoritative view of current thinking. If you would like a full listing of current and forthcoming titles, please visit our web site **www.chandospublishing.com** or contact Hannah Grace-Williams on email info@chandospublishing.com or telephone number +44 (0) 1865 884447.

New authors: we are always pleased to receive ideas for new titles; if you would like to write a book for Chandos, please contact Dr Glyn Jones on email gjones@chandospublishing.com or telephone number +44 (0)1865 884447.

Bulk orders: some organisations buy a number of copies of our books. If you are interested in doing this, we would be pleased to discuss a discount. Please contact Hannah Grace-Williams on email info@chandospublishing.com or telephone number +44 (0) 1865 884447.

Knowledge Management

An integrative approach

MELIHA HANDZIC AND
ALBERT Z. ZHOU

Chandos Publishing
Oxford • England

Chandos Publishing (Oxford) Limited
Chandos House
5 & 6 Steadys Lane
Stanton Harcourt
Oxford OX29 5RL
UK
Tel: +44 (0) 1865 884447 Fax: +44 (0) 1865 884448
Email: info@chandospublishing.com
www.chandospublishing.com

First published in Great Britain in 2005

ISBN:
1 84334 122 0 (paperback)
1 84334 123 9 (hardback)

© Meliha Handzic and Albert Z. Zhou, 2005

British Library Cataloguing-in-Publication Data.
A catalogue record for this book is available from the British Library.

Typeset by SPS Ltd. Printed in the UK and USA.

Contents

Preface

Knowledge has been widely recognised as a key competitive resource for organisations. As a result, how to better create, transfer and utilise knowledge has become an important concern for modern business administration. There is a growing demand for managerial and professional knowledge workers – with specialised knowledge management (KM) skills and capabilities to take the lead – and for KM initiatives to improve enterprise competitiveness in an ever-changing global environment.

This book focuses on basic KM concepts and their interrelationships. Most importantly, the book brings together diverse perspectives currently seen in the field of KM research and practice in a logical sequence incorporating the most relevant and representative examples into an integrated framework. It offers a comprehensive coverage of the KM phenomena including: KM frameworks, KM drivers, socio-technological enablers and processes, KM outputs and outcomes, as well as issues and challenges for KM. With its integrated and systematic approach to KM phenomena, the book contributes to achieving an objective and complete picture of the field.

The book begins with Chapter 1 presenting different perspectives on KM and bringing them together into an integrated framework that serves as a platform for structuring the rest of the book. Chapter 2 addresses major business drivers of KM including the nature of knowledge economy, knowledge organisation and knowledge work.

The four chapters in the second part of the book examine the four basic components of knowledge management and their relationships. Chapter 3 examines the role of various social and organisational factors including organisational culture, structure, leadership, rewards and incentives, and measurement, while Chapter 4 focuses on the role of information and communication technologies and systems in knowledge management processes. Chapter 5 examines four generic knowledge manipulation processes including knowledge creation, storage/retrieval, sharing/transfer and application, through which knowledge is created, modified, transferred and applied. Chapter 6 explores different conceptualisations of knowledge and presents a view of knowledge as an important personal and organisational asset.

The final part of the book addresses the various benefits and limitations of KM. Chapter 7 looks into performance outcomes from KM including knowledge preservation, improvements in the efficiency and effectiveness of business process, and most importantly innovation. The final chapter, as is appropriate, examines major issues and challenges facing KM practice and research, and suggests an agenda for future research and development.

It is hoped that the book will help students, individuals and organisations to better understand the benefits and limitations of KM. It is also hoped that the book will help managers to develop suitable KM solutions that will turn their intangible assets into tangible outcomes.

Acknowledgements

There are several people whom we would like to thank for their help and support in the process of writing this book. We owe an enormous debt to Sue Scott of the Law and Justice Foundation of NSW, Australia for her thorough review of the entire manuscript. We have benefited much from her rich practical experience in knowledge and information management. The quality of the content and style of the book would have been less good without her reading and editing. However, we bear responsibility for any shortcomings that the book may contain. We also thank the publisher Dr Glyn Jones for his enthusiasm about this book from the start and his professional approach throughout the project. Finally, thanks go to our families for always being there for us. Their love and support matters a great deal to us.

Meliha Handzic
Albert Z. Zhou

About the authors

Meliha Handzic is Associate Professor of Information Systems at Sarajevo School of Science and Technology, a partner of the University of Buckingham in the UK. She received her PhD in Information Systems from the University of New South Wales, where she was the Inaugural Leader of the Knowledge Management Research Group at the School of Information Systems, Technology and Management. Meliha's main teaching and research interests lie in the areas of knowledge management and decision support, with a particular focus on the processes and socio-technological enablers of knowledge creation, sharing, retention and discovery. She has published many papers on these topics in books, international journals and conference proceedings.

Currently Meliha is an active member of several professional societies and groups including IFIP TC8 and IAIM, is Regional Editor of *Knowledge Management Research and Practice* and serves on editorial boards and executive and programme committees for numerous international and national journals and conferences. Prior to joining academia, Meliha was an International Expert in Information Systems for the United Nations Development Programme in Asia and Africa, and also has had wide-ranging industrial experience in Europe.

Albert Z. Zhou is a statistician in the Economics, Research and Information Directorate within the NSW Department of Community Services, Australia. Beyond his professional career, Albert is a freelance KM researcher and writer. His research interests are in the areas of intellectual capital and knowledge management, with a special interest in the linkage between the two. He has written two books on KM and has had articles published in journals such as the *Journal of Intellectual Capital, Knowledge Management Research and Practice* and the *Journal of Information and Knowledge Management*. Albert was the recipient of Emerald Literati's 2004 Outstanding Paper Award for Excellence and is on the panel of reviewers for the *International Journal of Knowledge Management Research and Practice*. He is currently working toward the development of a theory of strategic management of knowledge and intellectual capital.

The authors may be contacted via the publishers.

Part 1
Introduction to KM

An integrated view of KM

Introduction

Over the last couple of years, knowledge management (KM) has become one of the most popular and important topics in academic research and management practice. This is clearly reflected in the large number of conferences, as well as special issues of journals and books published. This development has both its benefits and drawbacks. The main benefit can be seen in the positioning of knowledge as the most important production factor in the modern economy. The main drawback is that people from diverse disciplines all claim to do KM, but with very different understandings of the term. The objective of this book is to address some of the challenges brought about by the novel and complex nature of the field of KM.

Recent literature describes KM as the latest management response to the changing nature of the world economy. The emerging new economy is variously referred to as the third wave, the information age, knowledge-based economy or knowledge economy. Regardless of the terminology, what really matters is that a major transition is taking place in the world economy. This new economy is global, directly based on the production, distribution and use of knowledge in the development and distribution of products and services. It is also heavily reliant on information technology. For organisations competing in the new economy, the ability to identify and leverage their knowledge assets plays a critical role (Drucker, 1993; Stewart, 1997). Consequently, companies are facing challenges to better utilise their knowledge assets. Effective KM is seen as the key to survival and prosperity in the new economy.

However, while there is a wide recognition of the importance of KM for economic advancement or survival, there is very little shared understanding of the phenomenon itself. In their attempt to define KM, some authors adopt a process-orientated view of the phenomenon. Bhatt (2001) considers KM as a process of knowledge creation, validation, presentation, distribution and application. Malhorta (2000) sees it as the embodiment of the synergistic combination of data and information processing capacity of information technologies and the creative and innovative capacity of human beings. Others, like Bollinger and Smith (2001), define the objective of KM in terms of making the organisation act as intelligently as possible and realising the best value from its knowledge assets, by creating a learning organisation that is capable of measuring, storing and capitalising on the expertise of employees. Together, various KM definitions allude to the complexity of the interplay between people and technology in innovative organisational processes and activities in the pursuit of business objectives (Handzic and Hasan, 2003).

Recognising the existing confusion of terminology and cross-functional areas in practice of KM, our prime objective in this chapter is to investigate the relationship between diverse perspectives of KM, and to determine what is known about the fundamental concepts of this phenomenon to date.

Overview of current perspectives on KM

In order to make sense of the variety of perspectives of KM that exist in the literature, there have been a number of attempts to categorise or group them (Alavi and Leidner, 2001; Handzic, 2004; Holsapple and Joshi, 1999; McAdam and McCreedy, 1999). In this chapter, we use Earl's (2001) taxonomy shown in Table 1.1 as a context for discussing different types of strategies or schools of KM. The schools are divided into three general categories: technocratic, economic and behavioural.

Technocratic school of KM

The technocratic school of KM places emphasis on the role of information and communication technologies in KM. In Earl's (2001)

Table 1.1 Earl's taxonomy of schools of KM

Attribute	Technocratic			Economic	Behavioural		
	Systems	Cartographic	Engineering	Commercial	Organisational	Spatial	Strategic
Focus	Technology	Maps	Processes	Income	Networks	Space	Mindset
Aim	Knowledge bases	Knowledge directories	Knowledge flows	Knowledge assets	Knowledge pooling	Knowledge exchange	Knowledge capabilities
Unit	Domain	Enterprise	Activity	Know-how	Communities	Place	Business
Example	Xerox Shorko Films	Brain & Co AT&T	HP Frito-Lay	Dow Chemical IBM	BP Amoco Shell	Skandia British Airways	Skandia Unilever
Critical success factors	Content validation incentives to provide content	Content incentives to share knowledge networks information to connect people	Knowledge learning and Unrestricted distribution	Specialist teams and institutionalised process	Sociable culture, knowledge, intermediaries	Design for purpose and encouragement	Rhetoric Artefacts
Principal IT contribution	Knowledge-based systems	Profiles and directories on Internets	Shared database	Intellectual asset register and processing system	Groupware and intranets	Access and representational tools	Eclectic
Philosophy	Codification	Connectivity	Capability	Commercialisation	Collaboration	Contactivity	Consciousness

taxonomy, the technocratic category consists of the systems, cartographic and engineering schools.

The systems school focuses on formalised knowledge bases. In these systems, the knowledge of human experts is made explicit so that they can be used by non-expert workers. The cartographic school focuses on knowledge directories or yellow pages of experts that allow other workers to more easily locate the person who has the knowledge they need. In this case, knowledge is tacit and resides in experts' individual minds. The engineering school focuses on processes and knowledge flows. From the engineering school perspective, KM systems are designed to document knowledge processes and store best business practices. Data captured in shared databases, data warehouses and document management systems are used to support planning and decision-making to meet customers' needs.

The knowledge management systems framework developed by Hahn and Subramani (2000) is another model that fits well into the technocratic grouping. It identifies the following issues and challenges related to the utilisation of information and communication technologies for KM: the need to balance knowledge exploitation and exploration, overload and useful content, additional workload and accurate content. There is also a need for flexibility, evolutionary development and user acceptance of knowledge systems. The case study from the Australian construction company presented later in the chapter describes yet another example of the systems framework.

Economic school of KM

The economic school of thought of KM focuses on the notion of knowledge as an organisational asset. Sveiby's (1997) intangible assets monitor model is one of the first and best known representatives in this category. The human resources literature relies heavily on the intellectual capital (IC) grouping of KM models and frameworks, as does the accounting discipline's work on intangible assets. Essentially, these models are concerned with different types of organisational resources that are referred to as intellectual capital. They incorporate: employee competence (or human capital) that comprises the individual knowledge and skills; internal structures (or organisational capital) that involves the knowledge institutionalised as the organisational structures, processes and culture; and external structures (or customer capital) that consist of the company's brand names, relationships with customers and suppliers, its image and reputation.

From the IC perspective, KM aims to create and/or extract value from knowledge assets by maximising the interrelationship between different types of organisations' intellectual capital. In contrast, Earl's (2001) commercial category is more concerned with protecting and exploiting a firm's knowledge or intellectual assets to produce revenue. It emphasises the importance of patents and copyrights as means to protect these assets. It also suggests that since not all intellectual assets can be legally protected by a patent management system, the entire protection process should be addressed.

Behavioural school of KM

Earl's (2001) behavioural category consists of the organisational, spatial and strategic schools. The organisational school emphasises organisational structures that facilitate knowledge sharing and pooling. The essence of the organisational school is the pooling of knowledge by networked employees. The spatial school focuses on creating physical spaces for greater facilitation of knowledge exchange. Office space design maximises the opportunities for people to socialise with the expectation that this will lead to exchanges of knowledge. The organisational culture emphasises the sharing of knowledge. The strategic school emphasises knowledge as a competitive weapon. It sees KM as a firm's strategy.

Another model in this KM grouping that emphasises the dependence of knowledge on context is the concept of ba (the Japanese word for place) by Nonaka and Konno (1998). They suggested that four types of ba (originating, interacting, cyber and exercising) act as promoters of socialisation, externalisation, combination and internalisation (SECI) processes and so enabling knowledge creation. The concept of ba extends Nonaka's (1998) earlier SECI or spiral model that is perhaps the most frequently quoted and used model in the knowledge management literature. More detailed discussions about the SECI framework and the concept of ba are provided in Chapter 5.

In general, the behavioural group of models addresses issues of complexity, organisational culture and learning, change and risk management, and the support of communities of practice.

Case study 1.1

Australian construction company's KM framework

We present a case study of a KM framework in a real-world company as an example of a domain-specific framework in a practical context. The case organisation is an Australian commercial, residential, industrial and retail construction and real estate investment company. The core business of the organisation is project management and construction. The company offers a broad range of skills to clients across sectors. To structure the variety, depth and richness of knowledge accumulated over the years of experience in the construction industry, the company adopted the knowledge management framework shown in Figure 1.1. The company promotes the framework as a vehicle of harnessing organisational knowledge for reuse, learning and process improvement, and thus a source of competitive advantage.

The benefit of having such a framework is seen in the ability of the organisation to synthesise units of knowledge. This synthesis allows new knowledge to be created based on existing codified knowledge. Figure 1.1 shows how knowledge units (S, X and Y) can be part of different knowledge structures (A and B). A knowledge structure is defined as a collection of knowledge units. Two knowledge structures are depicted in Figure 1.1. Structure A includes the knowledge units P, Q, S, X and Y, and structure B includes R, S, X

Figure 1.1 The construction company's KM framework

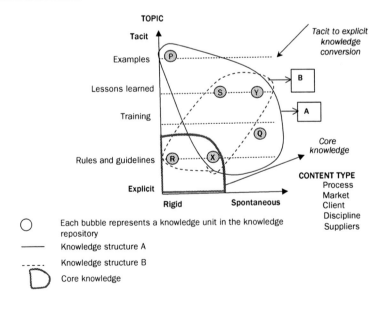

○ Each bubble represents a knowledge unit in the knowledge
   repository

─── Knowledge structure A

- - - - Knowledge structure B

⌐⌐ Core knowledge

and Y. The decisions on the inclusions of each structure are a result of many years of experience, arising from a deep understanding of how the business operates. Different facets of each knowledge structure are drawn from multiple employees who have been involved in different projects at different points of time.

The framework structures the company's knowledge along two dimensions: topics and content types. Each unit of knowledge (denoted by a bubble) describes a specific topic (vertical axis) and its corresponding content (horizontal axis). Topics describe the types (or forms) of knowledge such as examples, lessons learned, forms, rules and guidelines. These topics can be placed on a continuum depending on the level of explicitness of the knowledge. At one end of the spectrum, there is explicit knowledge (e.g. rules and guidelines) which is already codified and therefore is readily available to employees. On the other end, there is tacit knowledge, that which resides in the minds of people. At any one point of time, this explicit–tacit continuum allows us to distinguish how some pieces of knowledge are more explicit than others. Over time, the exact location of knowledge along the continuum may change because of the evolving nature of knowledge.

Each knowledge unit can fall under different categories, depending on its content type. Content types reflect the parts of the organisation the knowledge describes. Examples of content types are process, market, client, sectors and community of practice.

Content types can be placed along the rigid–spontaneous scale. Placement of content types is not fixed because it can change depending on the topic types. Rigid knowledge is inflexible and not readily changeable, while spontaneous knowledge typically arises from voluntary conversations that occur in a social or informal setting, and is more volatile.

Organisational knowledge management systems can contain a variety of knowledge units including rules, guidelines and lessons learned about both business processes and clients. For example, a collection of explicit knowledge consisting mainly of rules and guidelines forms the core knowledge of the organisation. This knowledge is based on business experience accumulated over decades. At one time, some parts of the core knowledge were tacit (e.g. examples and lessons learned). Over time, repeated experiences and the externalisation of knowledge held by individuals and project teams enabled this knowledge to become explicit and be part of the day-to-day business operations.

The development of the building services commissioning processes and resulting building services manual represents a good example of an evolving unit of knowledge. Thirty years ago, the technology and processes for commissioning building services (e.g. air conditioning, hydraulics, communications, fire protection and security) were not as they are now. Because of the tacitness and immaturity of this knowledge, it would reside in the outer quadrant of our graphical representation in Figure 1.1. Advances in technology and the attainment of maturity and experience in the commissioning processes have enabled the pioneering development of this manual in Australia in the late 1980s. This manual therefore represents a significant intellectual asset of the organisation and would form part of the core knowledge of the organisation. Moving from the outer quadrants to inside the core area is desirable as knowledge is captured (i.e. made explicit), stabilised and made independent of the individuals.

Source: Land, Land and Handzic (2002).

An integrated approach to KM

The above discussion on the groupings of KM approaches shows that KM frameworks can encompass a broad range of issues, methods and theories. A recent KM survey (Edwards et al., 2003) reveals the widespread belief that western theorists are more preoccupied with codified repositories and information processing as enablers of 'explicit' objective and systematic knowledge, while Eastern theorists, on the other hand, focus more on 'tacit' knowledge that people derive from their experiences and through knowledge sharing. Davenport and Prusak (1998) argued that the full power of knowledge can only be realised by taking a holistic approach to knowledge management.

Furthermore, Chae and Bloodgood (2004) suggested the need to look at KM dialectically to counter serious paradoxes that exist in KM due to competing unitary views of KM on concepts such as learning, organising and belonging. They identified key sources of learning paradoxes in the tensions between exploitation and exploration, purposeful and accidental learning. They related organising paradoxes to tensions between formal and informal approaches, control and autonomy, integration and differentiation. Finally, they saw paradoxes of belonging in tensions between cooperation and competition, community and self-interests.

The variation between different schools of thought on knowledge management is an indication of the many problems the concept poses. Accordingly, there is a need to develop frameworks that will provide KM researchers with a holistic view, common ground and consistent terminology, and units of analysis across a variety of settings. There is also a need to develop frameworks that can help practitioners to understand the sorts of KM initiatives or investments that are possible and to identify those that make sense in their context.

Recently, Handzic and Hasan (2003) have reviewed a number of projects worldwide that are working on integrated models of KM. Their review reveals that all integrated frameworks consider KM as a complex and multidimensional concept; synthesise the object and human perspectives of knowledge; view KM as both social and technological concept; and recognise the evolutionary and contextual nature of KM. In this chapter, we use the *driver-enabler-process-knowledge-outcome* model adapted from Handzic (2004) as a basis for discussing the fundamental concepts of KM in a holistic manner. This model builds on the author's earlier work (Handzic and Hasan, 2003) and essentially provides a missing link between technological, behavioural and economic schools of KM. The main contribution of the model is that it helps organise various individual factors in a more meaningful way. The main model components and their relationships are depicted in Figure 1.2.

Main components and relationships

First, the model recognises that KM is driven by forces from its surrounding external environment, and that any KM initiative must have

Figure 1.2   Driver-enabler-process-knowledge-outcome framework of KM

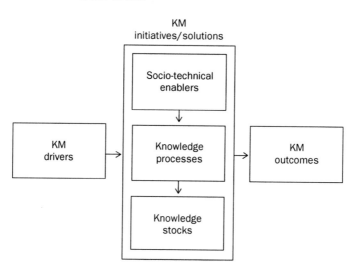

strategic intent as a guide. The Australian KM standard (AS 5037, 2003) describes drivers as strategic levers through which an organisation delivers its desired outcomes. It identifies operational excellence, stakeholder intimacy, service delivery, growth, sustainable profitability and risk mitigation among core strategic drivers found across for- and non-profit sectors. Becerra-Fernandez et al. (2004) distinguish four underlying trends – increasing domain complexity, accelerating market volatility, intensified speed of responsiveness and diminishing individual experience (due to high employee turnover) – that push managers to make better business decisions. Earl's (2001) strategic category provides further reinforcement of the view of knowledge as a competitive weapon and points to the importance of KM consciousness in a firm's business strategy.

Second, the model views KM solutions as configurations of organisational-technological knowledge enablers, knowledge processes and knowledge stocks. Supported by Nonaka and Konno's (1998) concept of ba, the model brings together the technology, maps, spatial and networks categories of Earl's (2001) technocratic and behavioural schools of KM.

Two classes of knowledge enablers are proposed: the organisational environment such as the organisational culture, leadership, organisational structure and measurement and the technological infrastructure including a wide range of information and communication technologies. The organisational environment is assumed to help create a knowledge-conducive climate and technological infrastructure to facilitate knowledge processes. Knowledge measurement or feedback suggests the need for continuous knowledge audits and adjustment of KM strategies over time.

The process component of the model covers various processes through which knowledge is moved and modified. This includes processes that develop new knowledge such as creative idea generation and mining of hidden patterns in captured data. It also includes processes that transfer existing knowledge via a person-to-person interaction, or through wider dissemination of captured and encoded knowledge in a person-to-document interaction. The underlying assumption is that the better the processes of knowledge generation, sharing, capture and discovery, the greater the likelihood that the knowledge needed will be available leading to more effective and innovative organisational performance.

The core of the integrated model is the concept of knowledge. From Earl's (2001) economic and Sveiby's (1997) intellectual capital perspectives, knowledge is seen as a valuable organisational asset. However, there are diverse views on what people perceive knowledge to be

(Handzic and Hasan, 2003). One view sees knowledge as an object that can be separated from its sources and context, codified and then stored in a computerised system. The other distinct view says that knowledge can only reside in people and that KM allows knowledge seekers to identify and communicate with knowledge sources in a connected environment for knowledge exchange. The integrated framework brings together human and object perspectives of knowledge by proposing a multi-dimensional view. Drawing from prior literature, it combines explicit and tacit know-what and know-how dimensions into a two-dimensional knowledge matrix based on whether knowledge resides in artefacts or people, and whether it is declarative or procedural by nature.

Finally, the integrated model includes a KM outcomes component that allows us to examine the impacts of KM on organisational performance. The Australian KM standard (AS 5037, 2003) identifies two principal benefits of undertaking KM: improved productivity and organisational efficiency, and the promotion of innovation. Becerra-Fernandez et al. (2004) classify benefits into impacts on people in terms of employee learning and satisfaction; impacts on processes including effectiveness, efficiency and innovation; impacts on products in the form of value-added and knowledge-based products; and direct and indirect impacts on organisational performance through advertising and demonstrating intellectual leadership in industry. Earl's (2001) economic school of KM suggests that when aligned with business strategy, KM may generate revenue and profit through the use of knowledge to create innovative and improved products and services. It may also generate sustainable competitive advantage by effective use of its accumulated intangible assets to develop and exploit other tangible resources better than the competitors.

Conclusion

This chapter identifies a variety of different perspectives of KM by reviewing and organising current KM literature. It then offers an integrated approach to structuring our thinking about KM as a way of reconciling individual views, and of providing researchers with a common language to communicate KM phenomena and practitioners with a means to better address the paradoxical world they confront. The integrated approach presented also serves as a basis for structuring the content of the remaining chapters in this book.

References

Alavi, M. and Leidner, D.E. (2001) 'Knowledge management and knowledge management systems: conceptual foundations and research issues', *MIS Quarterly*, 25 (1): 107–36.

AS 5037 (2003) *Interim Australian Standard: Knowledge Management.* Sydney: Standards Australia International.

Becerra-Fernandez, I., Gonzales, A. and Sabherwal, R. (2004) *Knowledge Management: Challenges, Solutions, and Technologies.* Upper Saddle River, NJ: Pearson Education.

Bhatt, G.D. (2001) 'Knowledge management in organisations: examining the interaction between technologies, techniques and people', *Journal of Knowledge Management*, 5 (1): 68–75.

Bollinger, A.S. and Smith, R.D. (2001) 'Managing organisational knowledge as a strategic asset', *Journal of Knowledge Management*, 5 (1): 8–18.

Chae, B. and Bloodgood, J.M. (2004) 'Paradoxes in knowledge management: a dialectic perspective', in *Proceedings of the Tenth Americas Conference on Information Systems*. New York, August, pp. 2284–94.

Davenport, T.H. and Prusak, L. (1998) *Working Knowledge.* Boston: Harvard Business School Press.

Drucker, P.F. (1993) *Post-Capitalist Society.* New York: Harper Business.

Earl, M. (2001) 'Knowledge management strategies: toward a taxonomy', *Journal of Management Information Systems*, 18 (1): 215–33.

Edwards, J., Handzic, M., Carlsson, S. and Nissen, M. (2003) 'Knowledge management research and practice: visions and directions', *Knowledge Management Research and Practice*, 1 (1): 49–60.

Hahn, J. and Subramani, M.R. (2000) 'A framework of knowledge management systems: issues and challenges for theory and practice', in *Proceedings of the International Conference on Information Systems, ICIS'2000*, Brisbane, Australia, pp. 302–12.

Handzic, M. (2004) *Knowledge Management through the Technology Glass.* Singapore: World Scientific.

Handzic, M. and Hasan, H. (2003) 'The search for an integrated KM framework', in H. Hasan and M. Handzic (eds), *Australian Studies in Knowledge Management*. Wollongong: UOW Press, pp. 3–34.

Holsapple, C.W. and Joshi, K.D. (1999) 'Description and analysis of existing knowledge management frameworks', in *Proceedings of the 32nd Hawaii International Conference on System Sciences*, pp. 1–15.

Land, L.P.W., Land, M. and Handzic, M. (2002) 'Retaining organisational knowledge: a case study of an Australian construction company', *Journal of Information and Knowledge Management*, 1 (2): 119–29.

Malhorta, Y. (2000) 'Knowledge management for E-business performance', *Information Strategy, The Executive Journal*, 16 (4): 5–16.

McAdam, R. and McCreedy, S. (1999) 'A critical review of knowledge management models', *Learning Organisation*, 6 (3): 91–100.

Nonaka, I. (1998) 'The knowledge creating company', in *Harvard Business Review on Knowledge Management*. Boston: Harvard Business School Press.

Nonaka, I. and Konno, N. (1998) 'The concept of ba: building a foundation for knowledge creation', *California Management Review*, 40 (3): 40–54.

Stewart, T.A. (1997) *Intellectual Capital: The New Wealth of Organisations*. New York: Doubleday.

Sveiby, K.-E. (1997) *The New Organizational Wealth*. San Francisco: Berrett-Koehler.

2

Drivers of KM

Introduction

Peter F. Drucker, praised as the father of modern management, says we live in a period of enormous social and economic change (Drucker, 2001). Furthermore, Nonaka (1998), one of the pioneers in the field of KM, claims that organisations increasingly inhabit 'chaotic' environments, where the link between cause and effect becomes difficult to discern, small changes can be amplified beyond comprehension and the future eludes prediction. In such environments, organisations live with an inherent ambiguity, while competing on the edge of stability and instability.

According to Nonaka, only two things are certain for these organisations – their own decomposition as product/service life cycles rapidly change, and the impossibility of focusing organisational futures around known strategic portfolios. Thus organisational survival will depend on ceaseless innovation and a capability to find opportunities for the exercise of new strategies. Raich (2000) argues that the increased complexity, uncertainty and surprises are brought about by a 'Bermuda triangle' of globalisation, transformation and digitalisation. In the following sections, we will take a closer look at these global trends and their economic, organisational and work-related aspects and outcomes.

Environmental forces driving KM

Global trends

National governments, international organisations like the World Trade Organisation (WTO) and market forces together are the main driving forces behind globalisation. The trend is also fuelled by the dramatic development of Internet technology and is further strengthened by a demand for the world to be part of the global community and integrated into the global economy. Global deregulation allows new competitors to enter previously protected national monopolies. Combined with the rapid development of networked services, this leads to hyper-competition. To succeed in an environment characterised by fierce competition and accelerated change, organisations need to better utilise their knowledge resources for competitive advantage and develop a greater ability to act and adapt.

Transformation from the traditional industrial economy to a knowledge-based economy is driven largely by the recognition that knowledge assets or IC, rather than financial capital, land or labour, are the major source of continued economic growth, value and improved standard of living. IC is intellectual material in its various forms that drives growth and value creation. It is the means of production in the knowledge economy and includes knowledge stored in patents, copyrights, corporate data warehouses, employees' brains, processes and information systems used in pursuit of improvements to core processes. The transformation process leads to a decline in relative importance of tangible assets, and demands a paradigm shift to relying on knowledge and intellectual capital (Guthrie, 2001).

Digitalisation is facilitated primarily by the explosion of new technologies. Advances in digital, wireless and optical technologies are creating a new communications capacity. In addition to text and numbers, almost everything – voice, sounds and graphics – can be digitised and transmitted through global networks. The demand for data communications is also growing, while the Internet, intranets and extranets are creating a boom in data traffic, and providing new business opportunities. However, the booming of data traffic is also generating an abundance of knowledge artefacts and hence posing great challenges to organisations' information management processes.

According to Raich (2000), the outcome from this change will be a different world, involving new ways of work, new organisational forms and a new, knowledge-based economy in which growth, value and an improving standard of living are inextricably tied to the creation and distribution of knowledge. In particular, the prevalence of information and communication technologies has resulted in the emergence of new means of work, production, shopping and education, increased codification of knowledge, and decreased costs of knowledge dissemination (ABS, 2002). Moreover, unrelenting technological change mixed with economic globalisation makes employee knowledge, skills and abilities become outdated rapidly (Hitt et al., 1994). These factors pose a great challenge for organisations to manage knowledge effectively. In this new environment, individuals and organisations need to devise ways to better acquire new knowledge and collaborate with each other to deal with increasing turbulence and speed of change.

Shifting economy

While every economy relies on knowledge as its base, the knowledge economy differs substantially from its predecessors. In traditional industrial economies, economic growth is explained by the basic production factors: land, labour and financial capital, and combinations thereof, all of which are in scarce supply (Toffler, 1991). Therefore, the bottleneck of economic growth rests on the scarcity of resources. In the knowledge economy, knowledge itself is for sale, and ideas are the main output or product of the major economic institutions. Stewart (2002), one of the prominent figures in the area of intellectual capital, suggests that the knowledge economy stands on three pillars: knowledge has become what we buy, sell and do; knowledge assets have become more important to firms than financial and physical assets; and we need new management techniques and new strategies to prosper. It is based on these three pillars that KM has blossomed and become one of today's management buzzwords.

According to Tiwana (2001), the knowledge economy has some distinct characteristics including knowledge centricity, increasing returns, network effects, accelerated change, transparency, customer loyalty, innovation, strategic alliances and products as experiences. Tiwana summarises these characteristics as follows:

- New economy is knowledge centric because services and non-physical as well as physical goods depend on knowledge for their production and distribution (e.g. news, consulting).

- Knowledge-based offerings demonstrate increasing returns. Once the first unit is produced at a significant cost, additional units can be produced at a near-zero cost (e.g. a piece of software).

- Network effects are visible in that the greater the market becomes for the knowledge-based offering, the more valuable that offering becomes. In this way, companies try to capture as much market share as possible and do so even at an initial loss (e.g. offer of free software).

- Rapid and unpredictable changes dominate. To cope with this, businesses must have adequate organisational and technological mechanisms to support speedy adaptation and knowledge application.

- As businesses become increasingly networked with others (e.g. customers, partners), their knowledge becomes more transparent and potent.

- Firms become differentiated based on the extent to which they can assimilate and mobilise their knowledge. Intimate knowledge of their customer base can help businesses provide tailored products and services and, in this way, develop and retain their customers' loyalty.

- Success in the new economy requires innovation in terms of new business processes, new business industries and new customers rather than the rearrangement of existing processes, industries and customers.

- Given the speed at which knowledge becomes obsolete, businesses must be capable of integrating new knowledge swiftly. This can be done through the formation of strategic partnerships between business partners and/or organisation members on a short-term and/or long-term basis.

- Products and services are increasingly perceived as experiences. This allows organisations to act as knowledge integrators, finding out and offering customers the customised (individualised) experiences they want and need.

Changing organisational forms

The term 'knowledge organisation' has been used to describe those organisations that rely on intellectual capital rather than tangible assets to obtain competitive advantage. Other metaphors used include agile production system, living organism, complex adaptive system, self-organising system, virtual organisation and knowledge-based organisation. Whatever the terminology used, a knowledge organisation effectively is an organisation that leverages and maximises knowledge in a value-added way.

A knowledge organisation can best be viewed as an intelligent, complex, adaptive system (Bennet and Bennet, 2003). It is complex because the system is composed of varying numbers of individual specialists called intelligent agents, who have multiple and complex relationships with the system and environment. It is adaptive because these intelligent agents direct and discipline their own performance through organised feedback from colleagues, customers and headquarters.

In general, an organisation's very existence is usually the result of a successful balance between the forces in their environment and their own creativity and adaptivity. Currently, knowledge organisations are at the forefront of organisational performance. These organisations recognise that the intelligent application of information and knowledge is an essential factor for success in the knowledge economy. Hence, they set up internal structures that mediate roles and relationships among people working toward a common goal. They focus on building favourable cultural environments conducive to tacit knowledge sharing. They also creatively make use of information technology to achieve high levels of efficiency and effectiveness.

In terms of successful knowledge organisations, the annual Global MAKE (most admired knowledge enterprises) study is worth noting. Started in 1998, the Global MAKE study is carried out by Teleos, a UK-based independent KM and IC research firm, to identify leading international knowledge organisations (Teleos, 2003). Winners are selected by a panel of examiners consisting of Global Fortune 500 senior executives and internationally respected KM experts.

In 2003, 20 organisations were adjudged the Global MAKE winners. As we can see from Table 2.1, the 2003 Global MAKE winners come from a variety of industrial sectors. Despite the diversity of background, these successful knowledge organisations have one thing in common, that is they create higher value and achieve growth through the creation and effective use of knowledge. According to Teleos's report, the shareholder value that these organisations created was twice as great as that of their competitors for the year 2003 alone. This is an impressive result, especially in view of the fact that this was achieved in a relatively tight economic environment.

Essentially, these organisations exhibit the following characteristics: creating knowledge-driven culture; developing knowledge workers through leadership; delivering knowledge-based products and/or

Table 2.1	2003 Global MAKE winners

Organisations	Industry
Toyota Motor	Automotive manufacturing
Buckman Laboratories	Chemicals
Accenture, Mckinsey & Company	Consulting
3M	Diversified
Canon, General Electric, Siemens, Xerox	Electronics and electrical equipment
World Bank	International development
Hewlett-Packard, Infosys Technologies, IBM, Microsoft	IT
Nokia	Network and communication equipment
BP, Royal Dutch/Shell	Oil and gas
Ernst & Young, PricewaterhouseCoopers	Professional services
Amazon.com	Speciality retailer

Source: Teleos (2003).

services; maximising IC; creating an environment for collaborative knowledge sharing; creating a learning organisation; delivering value based on customer knowledge; and transforming organisational knowledge into shareholder value.

Apparently, certain organisations are more knowledge intensive than others. For example, organisations which provide business and professional services (BPSs), such as KPMG Consulting and McKinsey & Co., are typical examples of knowledge organisations. These firms are closely associated with the overall economic performance of the knowledge economy. They have a dynamic relationship with many other sectors of the economy and add considerable value. BPSs include a range of services – from legal, accounting, engineering and architecture professions to business management consulting and computer services. Firms in this sector offer expertise and solve problems for their clients. Hence, the ability to transform knowledge into valuable advice is what defines the role of business and professional services.

Closely associated with a knowledge organisation is the concept of a learning organisation. A learning organisation is an organisation skilled at creating, acquiring and transferring knowledge, and at modifying its behaviour to reflect new knowledge and insights so that the entire firm will learn while it works and is able to adapt quickly to market changes and other environmental perturbations. Hence, a knowledge organisation must of necessity become a learning organisation. Emerging in the early 1990s, the idea of learning organisation provided a way forward for organisations operating in an environment of rapid change. In the words of Peter M. Senge, named as a 'Strategist of the Century' by the *Journal of Business Strategy* in 1999, a learning organisation is a place where people continually expand their capacity to create the results they truly desire, where new and expansive patterns of thinking are nurtured, where collective aspiration is set free and where people are continually learning how to learn together (Senge, 1990). To achieve these ends, these organisations use systems thinking, personal mastery, mental models, shared vision and team learning.

A learning organisation must possess some distinct characteristics, such as systematic problem-solving, experimentation, learning from past experience, learning from others and transferring knowledge. The way to build a learning organisation is to first foster an environment that is conducive to learning, then open up boundaries to stimulate the informal exchange of ideas, and finally create formal learning forums and programmes with explicit learning goals tailored to business needs. One important objective for building a learning organisation is to develop and/or create new knowledge. Nonaka (1998) once characterised knowledge-creating companies as places where inventing new knowledge is not a specialised activity, but a way of behaving, indeed a way of being, in which everyone is a knowledge worker. The way to achieve this is to use metaphors, encourage dialogue and make tacit ideas explicit.

While information and communication technology is not necessary to create a knowledge organisation, the use of advanced technologies can transform the way the whole business works. Modern communications technology virtually eliminates distance as a barrier in many types of work and enables different entities to join together to provide goods and services. Each entity takes advantage of the capabilities of another entity without having to physically link to it. By contributing their core competencies, these entities make collaborative teamwork across great distances a reality. People can work together on new products and services even if they are located on different continents. Martin (1996) terms this a 'cybercorp', a totally virtual organisation based on the capabilities of modern communications, i.e. the Internet and network technologies. Typically, a virtual organisation consists of three fundamental parts: knowledge professionals and workers who possess core competencies; relationships and networks of people including partners, suppliers and customers grouped around a common brand; and a culture based on cooperation and collaboration that permeates throughout global networks that are linked electronically.

While many will agree that most organisations manage their knowledge to some extent, the following list provides some typical characteristics of organisations that require a KM programme to create and sustain their business success.

Profile of organisations that typically need KM:

- Knowledge-intensive work
- Geographically dispersed
- Multiple business units
- Multiple disciplines and levels
- Large number of users
- Wide range of performances
- High staff turnover with resulting potential for knowledge loss
- Downsized industries
- Short product cycles
- Highly innovative companies
- Customer service feedback network
- High R&D budgets
- Learning curve has a significant impact on cost

Knowledge work

In knowledge organisations, the bulk of the workforce is engaged in so-called knowledge work. The term 'knowledge work' was coined back in the 1960s by Drucker when he was discussing the role of knowledge in organisations. Generally, the term refers to the production and reproduction of information and knowledge. Although the term is widely used, there is still a confusion about its meaning. Schultze (2003) explores knowledge work from three different perspectives: the economic perspective, the labour process perspective and the work practice perspective.

- The economic perspective emphasises how knowledge work differs from other types of work in terms of the nature of knowledge possessed and produced by knowledge workers. Knowledge work assumes the possession of the mostly abstract, theoretical and esoteric knowledge gained through formal education. It also suggests that knowledge workers have to produce new knowledge rather than just manipulate existing knowledge.

- The labour process perspective concerns itself with the formation and composition of a new class of white-collar workers between the proletariat and bourgeoisie who perform managerial, professional and clerical tasks. The work performed by white-collar workers is characterised by a scientific base, formal education, autonomy, ethical rules, culture, client orientation, social sanction and authorisation.

- The work practice perspective focuses on the work that knowledge workers do and classifies it into knowledge production and knowledge reproduction. Reproduction includes transfer and application. Specific processes and practices that form part of knowledge work include generating new knowledge and interpreting and representing it, as well as expressing, monitoring, translating and networking.

Given that knowledge work involves the production and reproduction of knowledge that has important economic value for the organisation, effective knowledge management is seen as vital in improving knowledge work. As we will see in the following chapters, there are various technological and organisational solutions that can be applied within an overall KM strategy, to develop an organisational capability and improve the application of knowledge in the collective interest of its stakeholders.

Main reasons for adopting KM

Consistent with our emphasis on drivers of KM, we focus our discussion in this section on the main reasons why organisations consider knowledge management and how they move towards adopting it. A mini-case study is provided at the end of this chapter, illustrating what motivated McKinsey's KM journey even when the concept of KM had not yet surfaced.

Typical reasons for embarking on KM:

- Limited access to outside knowledge
- Poor links with customers, vendors and strategic alliances
- Poor understanding of changing business and industry dynamics
- Stagnating skills
- Ineffective development of new products and services
- Little organisational knowledge
- Breakthrough ideas not leveraged across the organisation
- Available information not used 'smartly'

For example, a recent survey that examined the status of KM practices in US companies found that the three top reasons US firms adopt KM are: (1) retaining the expertise of employees; (2) enhancing customer satisfaction with the company's products; and (3) increasing profits or revenues. Other reasons mentioned by Becerra-Fernandez et al. (2004) include beneficial impacts on people such as improved employee learning and satisfaction, process efficiency and effectiveness, value-added and knowledge-based products, and improved overall organisational financial performance and competitive advantage.

While there may be many different individual reasons for starting knowledge management initiatives in organisations, Von Krogh et al. (2000) categorised them into three broad classes: (1) minimising risk; (2) improving efficiency; and (3) enabling innovation.

If the prime motive for knowledge management is minimising risk, the response typically involves identifying and holding on to the core competencies that the company has. Thus risk minimisation is closely related to knowledge initiatives aimed at locating and capturing valuable company knowledge. In most organisations, people have been recognised as key holders of valuable knowledge. Therefore identifying, locating and capturing what is known by individuals and groups of employees are of critical importance for business survival.

In today's complex economy, businesses are constantly confronted with the need to operate more efficiently in order to stay competitive and satisfy increasing market demands. Improving efficiency usually relates to knowledge initiatives for transferring experiences and best practices throughout the organisation in order to avoid unnecessary reinvention and to reduce cost. Technology often plays an important role in achieving efficiency improvements. Companies are now under greater pressure than ever from their customers to deliver solutions and services faster and cheaper. Therefore practitioners need to turn their attention to new methods and tools that can improve their processes for achieving enhanced efficiency and sustaining competitive advantage.

In addition to minimising risk and improving efficiency, effective knowledge management enables innovation. New products and services resulting from the application of knowledge may bring profound changes in the way businesses operate and compete in the new economy. The unifying thread among various theoretical views is the perception that innovation is the key driver of an organisation's long-term economic success. Innovation of products, processes and structures has been assessed as a critical component in business success in the twenty-first century. Typically, innovative organisations focus on both new knowledge and knowledge processes. They constantly engage and motivate people, creating the overall context to enable knowledge creation.

Successful organisations, such as the Global MAKE winners, take a strategic view of knowledge, formulate knowledge visions, tear down knowledge barriers, develop new corporate values and trust, catalyse and coordinate knowledge creation, manage the various contexts involved, develop a conversational culture, globalise local knowledge and localise global knowledge.

Case study 2.1

McKinsey

McKinsey & Co., founded in 1926, is now one of the world's best-known professional service firms. From its very early existence, McKinsey was dedicated to the mission of helping its clients make lasting and substantial improvements in their performance. By the late 1960s, McKinsey was a highly respected firm, enjoying success both domestically and internationally.

In the 1970s, the business environment in which McKinsey operated was undergoing a rapid change. A troubled world economy and social unrest undermined confidence. The business consultancy sector was facing increasing competitive pressure. Consulting firms were competing for the most attractive customers and the best graduates and employees. Firms were forced to differentiate themselves from other competitors by developing their expertise in the functional areas in company practice.

This meant that the traditional general approach to consulting was no longer effective, and consultants' expertise and specialisation became more and more critical. Furthermore, specialist regional knowledge and knowledge of the internationalisation process were also in demand due to the increasing pressure of internationalisation.

To address these challenges, McKinsey went through a process of introspection and reinvention. One outcome of this process was a substantial investment in knowledge development, particularly in the firm's key areas of expertise, strategy and organisation. These include the creation of Clientele Industry Sectors cutting across geographic boundaries, Centers of Competence building on existing areas of management expertise, and the development of a knowledge infrastructure throughout the whole organisation.

As a means of developing expertise, McKinsey established some special forms of 'practices' – think-tanks. A think-tank is actually an internal group of experts within the company. Today, these groups focus on developing their expertise in functional divisions (manufacturing etc.) for selected branches of industry (cars, banks) and on areas currently of special interest (e.g. Eastern Europe).

In addition to carrying out normal project work, experienced consultants have the responsibility to summarise and extract valuable knowledge from the projects in which they are involved and communicate it to others. This creates an excellent opportunity for young consultants and those with less experience to gain sound knowledge of a special area and to apply it to suitable projects. For instance, members of the 'energy' practice work on visions and concepts for the energy industry of tomorrow. When the project is completed, their experience is then summarised in condensed form as 'lessons learnt' and is made available to the whole organisation.

Sources: Bartlett (2000) and Probst, Raub and Romhardt (2000).

Conclusion

This chapter attempts to provide an understanding of the major forces driving KM. It identifies the chaotic business environment with increased complexity, ambiguity and uncertainty as the ultimate driving force of KM. It then describes various environmental aspects including global trends, shifting economies, new ways of organising and the growing importance of knowledge work. The chapter also identifies some typical reasons why organisations consider and move to knowledge management such as risk minimisation, process improvement and innovation.

However, not many organisations are able to manage knowledge effectively. Empirical studies in Australia and overseas reveal that few organisations are currently effective in leveraging knowledge to improve performance (Chase, 1997; Zhou and Fink, 2003). It seems that the greatest challenge for many organisations is to move in a knowledge-enabling direction by consciously and deliberately addressing knowledge management.

References

ABS (2002) *Measuring a Knowledge-based Economy and Society: An Australian Framework* (Discussion paper). Canberra: Australian Bureau of Statistics.

Bartlett, C.A. (2000) *McKinsey & Company: Managing Knowledge and Learning*, Vol. 9. Boston: Harvard Business School, pp. 357–96.

Becerra-Fernandez, I., Gonzales, A. and Sabherwal, R. (2004) *Knowledge Management: Challenges, Solutions, and Technologies*. Upper Saddle River, NJ: Pearson Education.

Bennet, D. and Bennet, A. (2003) 'The rise of the knowledge organisation', in C.W. Holsapple (ed.), *Handbook on Knowledge Management*, Vol. 1. Germany: Springer, pp. 5–20.

Chase, R.L. (1997) 'The knowledge-based organisation: an international survey', *Journal of Knowledge Management*, 1 (1): 38–49.

Davenport, T.H., De Long, D.W. and Beers, M.C. (1998) 'Successful knowledge management projects', *Sloan Management Review*, Winter: 43–57.

Drucker, P.F. (2001) *The Essential Drucker: Selections from the Management Works of Peter F. Drucker*. Oxford: Butterworth-Heinemann.

Guthrie, J. (2001) 'The management, the measurement and the reporting of intellectual capital', *Journal of Intellectual Capital*, 2 (1): 27–41.

Hitt, M.A., Hoskisson, R.E., Harrison, J.S. and Summers, T.P. (1994) 'Human capital and strategic competitiveness in the 1990s', *Journal of Management Development*, 13 (1): 35–46.

Martin, J. (1996) *Cybercorp: The New Business Revolution*. New York: Amacom.

Nonaka, I. (1998) 'The knowledge creating company', in *Harvard Business Review on Knowledge Management*. Boston: Harvard Business School Press.

Probst, G.J.B., Raub, S. and Romhardt, K. (2000) *Managing Knowledge*. Chichester: Wiley.

Raich, M. (2000) *Managing in the Knowledge Based Economy*. Zurich, Switzerland: Raich Ltd.

Schultze, U. (2003) 'On knowledge work', in C.W. Holsapple (ed.), *Handbook on Knowledge Management*, Vol. 1. Berlin: Springer, pp. 43–58.

Senge, P. (1990) *The Fifth Discipline: The Art and Practice of the Learning Organisation*. London: Century Business.

Stewart, T.A. (2002) *The Wealth of Knowledge: Intellectual Capital and the 21st Century Organisation*. Nicholas Brealey.

Teleos (2003) *2003 Global Most Admired Knowledge Enterprises: Executive Summary*. Available at: *http://www.knowledgebusiness .com* (accessed 15 August 2003).

Tiwana, A. (2001) *The Essential Guide to Knowledge Management*. Upper Saddle River, NJ: Prentice Hall.

Toffler, A. (1991) *Powershift: Knowledge, Wealth and Violence at the Edge of the 21st Century*. New York: Bantam Books.

Von Krogh, G., Ichijo, K. and Nonaka, I. (2000) *Enabling Knowledge Creation*. New York: Oxford University Press.

Zhou, A. and Fink, D. (2003) 'Knowledge management and intellectual capital: an empirical examination of current practice in Australia', *Knowledge Management Research and Practice*, 1 (2): 86–94.

Part 2

KM components and relationships

3

Organisational enablers of KM

Introduction

Knowledge can't be effectively managed without management's attention to a set of organisational attributes, including organisational culture, leadership, structure, incentives and rewards, and measurement. The role of these organisational factors lies primarily in creating an organisational environment conducive to effective knowledge management processes.

To create a positive knowledge creating and sharing environment, managers need to propose, select and design organisational interventions to support knowledge processes within an organisation. It is important that managers are able to identify and appraise those important organisational factors that influence the success of KM activities in order to implement changes.

This chapter examines how organisational culture, leadership, structure, incentives and rewards, and measurement act as major knowledge catalysts that facilitate the processes of knowledge creation and transfer.

Organisational culture

Organisational culture is widely recognised as one of the most important enablers or inhibitors of KM. As such, implementing KM requires a good understanding of the organisation's culture. Since organisational culture has a profound effect on the achievement of strategy and outcomes, a knowledge project only works in a favourable cultural environment. 'If the cultural soil isn't fertile for a knowledge project', say Davenport, De Long and Beers (1998), 'no amount of technology, knowledge content, or good project management practices will make the effort successful' (p. 53).

Research in Australia showed that while organisations perceived KM more from the cultural perspective rather than from the structural perspective, they did not practice as they preached (Zhou and Fink, 2003b). The reason for such a contradiction may be due to organisations' inability to create and maintain a knowledge culture, or that behavioural change to favour KM does not easily take place in a short time-frame. Therefore, many KM researchers and practitioners point out that the cultural change required to implement KM is the most challenging issue in IC and KM practice (Chase, 1997; Rumizen, 2002; Zhou and Fink, 2003b).

If the organisational culture is strong and supports knowledge sharing and innovation, it will make a positive impact on both individual and collective behaviour. This may be manifested in interpersonal behaviour, such as interaction and collaboration, or in the form of experimentation performed by creative and innovative individuals in order to solve problems. The attitude and actions of top management will impact on the effectiveness of culture, especially when the decisions from management contradict written policy. If the organisation aims to develop an innovative and knowledge-friendly culture, top management must commit to deliver and consistently act on that (the role of leadership is discussed separately in the next section).

Organisational culture may be explicitly expressed in the form of written strategic plans and policies or implicitly expressed in the words and behaviours of its employees. For example, knowing when to act and how to act is mostly determined by observing and following other people in the organisation.

Leidner (1999) observes that systems designed to facilitate KM are often seen to clash with corporate culture and therefore have limited impact. It is essential for organisations to develop an organisational environment conducive to tacit knowledge sharing, rather than just simply connecting people with information (Junnarkar and Brown, 1997). If employees are not willing to share their tacit knowledge, such knowledge is of little value to the organisation. Hence, the success of KM systems depends on an appropriate match with organisational culture, in particular with subcultures and individual cultures (Leidner, 1999).

Quite often, knowledge sharing between employees doesn't take place voluntarily, especially in a cultural environment viewing knowledge as a commodity, a competitive power, or a source of identity or security (Knights, 1995). Many KM initiatives, therefore, aim to generate cultural change so that employees will have the right attitudes or skills to adapt to the desired knowledge creating and sharing environment. However, since organisational culture takes years to evolve, it would be naive to expect cultural change to happen overnight. Trust must be developed in the first instance and must pervade all levels in the organisation. Only after that can management align KM initiatives with core organisational values (after carefully assessing their organisational culture) (Elliott and O'Dell, 1999). The following case study describes how a climate of openness and trust permeated among employees at Chaparral Steel, the tenth-largest US steel producer.

Case study 3.1

Chaparral Steel

Chaparral Steel promotes a climate of openness and shared responsibility. The company believes that collaboration is essential and must be reinforced. It also believes risk-taking is an essential part of knowledge acquisition and allows for mistakes made by employees in the process of pursuing innovative solutions.

At Chaparral Steel, there are no assigned parking spaces and no different coloured uniforms or hats reflecting titles or positions. The company dining room is a local diner and only two levels separate the CEO from operators in the mill.

Employees take responsibility for daily operations and solve any given problem on-site. They chip in and work together when solutions are needed. They collaborate to improve operations, develop new operating practice and create new technology. As a result, innovations occur so rapidly that they almost overlap. For example, when Chaparral designed its new steel I-beams, it worked with a German company that made moulds through which the hot steel would be poured. When the German company called to inform Chaparral that it had finished a prototype on schedule, the steel company told them to dismantle it and rebuild it from a new, improved design already completed by Chaparral. Management consider the $40,000 mould not a waste, but an investment in quick and improved innovation.

On another occasion, the caster for the company's new steel I-beams kept bursting its cooling hoses. Operators, a welder, foremen and even a buyer immediately gathered at the site of the problem to discuss the situation. They then scattered to make phone calls to vendors and experts. Very soon service people arrived and the problem was solved far more quickly than if only one person had been responsible for the device.

Chaparral also believes that locating all workers in the same place allows many 'accidental' meetings to occur and facilitates cross-fertilisation of ideas. Employees are not afraid to ask others for help. They are encouraged to add their own input to any ongoing project, and no one is punished for an idea that does not work. Operating problems are investigated to find out what can be learnt. In 1986, a medium-section mill superintendent encouraged the purchase of a $1.5 million machine for cutting finished beams. But the machine's magnetic fields attracted pieces of metal from yards around, including pens and watches. Even though this was a high-cost mistake, Chaparral viewed this as a lesson learnt. Today, the mill superintendent is vice president of operations.

Sources: Leonard-Barton (1995) and Wiig (1999).

Leadership

Leadership is one of the most important managerial influences on KM, as it is a critical success factor in implementing the cultural, organisational and technical change required. Control and coordination are also discussed briefly in this section as they are regarded as other important managerial influences (Holsapple, 2003). The adoption of KM in an organisation requires strong leadership to guide it towards managing and using its knowledge resource for maximum benefit. This is demonstrated in the case of Skandia (see Case study 3.2 below). While there may be several potential knowledge leadership roles in functions and teams as discussed in the next section, it is usually the CEO who establishes the mandate for KM activity and communicates its importance and the need for change.

The distinguishing characteristic of leadership is that of being a catalyst through inspiring, mentoring, setting examples, listening and engendering trust and respect. KM requires individuals and team leaders with a diverse range of skills, attributes and capabilities to manage and motivate change. These include strong interpersonal, communication and change management skills, an understanding of the business, technological expertise and the ability to build relationships.

Case study 3.2

Skandia AFS

Skandia Assurance & Financial Services (Skandia AFS) is a federation of savings organisations that operates in the United Kingdom, the United States, Columbia, Spain, Switzerland, Luxembourg, Germany and Hong Kong. It is among a handful of organisations in the world that have taken an active role in establishing frameworks for measuring and reporting intellectual capital – the so-called Skandia value scheme and Skandia Navigator. Skandia's work has attracted the attention of the US Securities and Exchange Commission (SEC) and the Financial Accounting Standards Board (FASB). Skandia's achievement has been a major inspiration for companies around the world aiming to visualise their invisibles.

The man who drove Skandia's IC movement is Leif Edvinsson, the world's first Director of Intellectual Capital appointed at Skandia AFS back in 1991. Edvinsson was asked 'to devise ways of describing the hidden values and develop an intellectual capital management model' for Skandia AFS. Furthermore, in order to 'systematically develop intellectual capital information and accounting systems, which can then be integrated with ... traditional financial accounting', another new role was created – an intellectual capital controller was appointed in 1993. Skandia's intellectual capital controller is the embodiment of Lusch and Harvey's (1994) 'Off-Balance-Sheet Controller', who monitors and analyses the assets that do not appear on traditional accounting balance sheets.

Sources: Edvinsson (1997) and Supplement to Skandia's Annual Report (1994).

Control

Control is concerned with ensuring that the required resources are available in sufficient quality and quantity, subject to required security. Two critical issues are protection and quality of knowledge resources. Protection of knowledge resources involves protecting knowledge resources from loss, obsolescence and unauthorised exposure and modification. Approaches include legal protection, social protection and technological protection (Holsapple, 2003).

Quality management provides tools and techniques that build quality into KM processes and practices. These include strategic policy and planning processes, development and management of people, design and improvement of product and service processes, documentation of policies, procedures and processes, and measurement of costs, performance and satisfaction.

Coordination

Coordination refers to managing dependencies among activities, and it involves determining what knowledge activities to perform, who to perform them and what knowledge resources to use. Essentially, coordination aims to harmonise activities by managing dependencies among knowledge resources, among knowledge activities, between knowledge and other resources and between resources and activities. Suggested coordination approaches include linking reward structures to knowledge sharing, establishing communications channels for sharing and constructing programmes to encourage learning (Holsapple, 2003).

For example, an innovation programme may provide employees with ways of suggesting creative ideas for improving the business, for identifying business opportunities, for reducing rework or for providing benefits to more than one business unit or the organisation as a whole. This is not to say that other aspects of management are not important. A successful innovation programme depends also on the commitment, culture, motivation and active involvement of all levels in the business.

Organisational structure

Recent research into the role of organisational structure in organisations revealed that it played a more important role than organisational culture and IT in the process of knowledge creation and sharing (Zhou and Fink, 2003b). This suggests that organisations are able to make use of a variety of organisational forms to create an environment to support collaboration and knowledge sharing. Not surprisingly, team-based, networked and systemic organisational structures offer the ability for individuals to work together across the organisation through engagements in KM initiatives. In contrast, bureaucratic structures that emphasise hierarchies and command and control over individuals discourage innovation. The following case study illustrates how a circle structure works for a manufacturing company – Harley-Davidson Inc.

Case study 3.3

Harley-Davidson Inc.

Whereas most manufacturing companies adopt a pyramid-style structure with rigid hierarchies, Harley-Davidson Inc. has taken a different approach. Instead of a pyramid structure with different functional departments strictly separated, Harley uses the circle – three circles to be exact. They are called the Create Demand Circle, the Produce Products Circle and the Support Circle. Most importantly, the circles overlap, with the marketing and sales functions in Create Demand overlapping and integrating with the engineering and manufacturing of Produce Products. Both these circles in turn overlap with the administrative and support functions in the Support Circle.

In the centre, where three circles intersect, is another circle called the Leadership and Strategy Council. This is not just another name for senior management. Rather, the council consists of the CEO plus six managers elected by their peers from the three circles. Each of the three circles gets to nominate three people, who can come from any circle. The six people with the highest number of votes are given a two-year term. The Leadership and Strategy Council looks across the other three circles and reviews strategies, plans and policies across the entire organisation. Not surprising, such an organisational structure encourages participation and collaboration among members within and between circles.

Source: Imperato (1997).

A networked organisational structure supported by net-based information and communication technologies encourages open communication and enables members of the network to get access to the right information at the right time for the right purpose (Zhou and Fink, 2003a). This is especially important for those organisations competing in the global market. An internally networked structure allows the knowledge (e.g. experience, expertise and lessons learnt) contributed by members in one location to be accessible by others elsewhere. By the same token, an externally networked structure enables organisations to acquire and extract external information and knowledge from customers, business partners and other stakeholders.

Communities of practice

One emerging form currently being widely adopted by organisations to facilitate knowledge transfer and sharing are communities of practice

(CoPs). CoPs are groups in which two or more people regularly engage in sharing and learning based on common interests (Lesser and Storck, 2001). These communities are established to provide value to organisations. They improve business performance by fostering an environment with shared mental models, common understanding, high levels of trust and mutual obligation (Lesser and Storck, 2001). Such an environment is important for effective person-to-person interactions to take place. It leads to effective knowledge sharing among community members.

Trust, group norms and a sense of common identity are all important factors in building a community of practice. This approach to organisational structuring advocates the formation of centres of expertise for each knowledge domain, discipline or subject matter speciality. As such, communities of practice can be organised around geographic areas, client industries, types of service, practice specialisations and so on. They can also be structured around projects and related activities.

Within a community, organisations often use electronic discussion facilities to transfer tacit knowledge from individuals to a knowledge repository (Davenport et al., 1998). In an electronic discussion, a single question may attract many responses and/or may trigger new questions for further discussion. Also, responses to requests posted are accessible to the whole of the group which has no limit on size and whose members may not be co-located. The benefits from using this approach are obvious. As Sharratt and Usoro (2003) put it, 'through the shared perspective, common language and context of OLCs [online communities], individuals are able to help resolve problems by sharing what they know'.

The emergence of OLCs or virtual communities is the result of the rapid development and prevalence of Internet and group-support technologies (e.g. Lotus Notes or Microsoft's Exchange). An effective way to create OLCs is to develop a multimedia-based virtual platform where these communities can be introduced as needed. Basically, this platform is a virtual construct using the corporate intranet or the Internet. The same platform can be used to link communities across companies. (These technologies will be discussed in more detailed in the next chapter.) Virtual communication adds a new dimension to person-to-person interaction.

Although virtual communication is becoming a popular mode of interaction, many agree that face-to-face conversation remains the most effective method of knowledge transfer. Hence, in addition to utilising information technologies for virtual interaction, some organisations pay attention to the design of physical office space to create a supportive work environment for knowledge sharing and creation. The total work area can be configured into a culturally encouraging working environment. Tea rooms, hot spots or coffee stations provide social spaces that allow ideas to arise from informal contact and conversations among different groups of people within the organisation. Seating staff identified as knowledge experts at key interaction points can also stimulate communication and collaboration.

Regardless of what form of interaction is used, regular cross-team meetings can foster innovation or the sharing of lessons learnt. Strategic conversations provide a valuable means for idea generation. They can contribute particularly to planning, by connecting and integrating diverse perspectives of the organisation and its environment. Storytelling is another valuable technique that may be used to describe complex issues, explain events, present perspectives and communicate experiences.

Roles and responsibilities of KM professionals

Having a supportive organisational structure for KM also means establishing a set of KM roles and positions within the organisation. An organisation may seek to appoint a particular individual to be responsible for KM. This could be at the senior executive level or as managers and facilitators at team levels. These individuals may assist in smoothing knowledge flows and enhancing the quality of knowledge objects.

Currently, there are three distinct categories of KM-related job titles and roles found in organisations. These three categories are:

1. *Knowledge manager.* The knowledge manager is primarily concerned with the knowledge needs of the organisation.

2. *Knowledge engineer.* Knowledge engineers, with various specialisations, advise knowledge managers on what can be done given the current 'state of the art'.

3. *Knowledge scientist.* Knowledge scientists then show others what would be possible if they were willing to try.

An increasing number of organisations have appointed executives with the titles of 'chief knowledge officer' (CKO), 'chief learning officer' (CLO) and 'director of intellectual capital' (DIC). ITword.com reported in 2003 that one in four large global firms had appointed a chief knowledge (or learning) officer (Essex, 2003).

A CKO is typically charged with gathering knowledge from a firm's geographically, functionally and intellectually dispersed divisions and orchestrating its use wherever it is needed. A CKO, like the one established at Ernst & Young, works at capturing and leveraging structured knowledge, using information technology to drive the process.

A CLO, on the other hand, is more overtly concerned with training and education, and HR, as opposed to IS, as a key enabler. At Coca-Cola, the job is described as 'creating and supporting an environment in which learning and applying what we learn is a daily priority'.

A DIC, like the one at Dow Chemical, tends to focus more on converting and/or extracting knowledge into revenues and profits.

Sources: Davenport (1996) and Ward (1996).

Results of a recent survey by McKeen and Staples (2000) of knowledge managers from US and Canadian organisations reveal the following profile of a 'typical' knowledge manager, including his or her typical individual characteristics and typical knowledge management roles:

- highly educated;
- already a seasoned organisational performer and chosen for the knowledge management position based on their proven performance;
- a 'researcher' – seeks new knowledge, likes to learn;
- attracted to 'being at the forefront of something new and exciting';
- motivated more by a challenge than a formal power;
- receives intrinsic rewards from helping others – some altruism and/or evangelism;
- a risk-taker – sometimes a maverick;
- sees knowledge management as a way to 'make a mark within the organisation'.

The snapshot of knowledge managers' characteristics and activities presented suggests that they are well-educated and experienced individuals, whose primary goal is to guide their organisations towards managing knowledge for maximum benefit, and who see changing people's behaviour as the key challenge. This self-reported picture can serve as a starting point in helping us to better understand the current practice of knowledge managers, as well as the potential of their role in organisations.

Having said that, it should be noted that KM roles are a relatively new phenomenon, and there is still no consensus about what roles they should play in an organisation and what competencies and skills they need to have to play these roles. Compared with the chief information officer (CIO) who has a well-defined role in managing technology systems in many companies, including such giants as Cigna, Coca-Cola, General Electric and Hewlett–Packard, a chief knowledge officer has a much broader and less clear space to navigate.

Moreover, although KM roles are said to be somewhat unique and beneficial (McKeen and Staples, 2000), some companies find it difficult to maintain them as there is usually substantial cost involved (Davenport et al., 1998). The KM roles are still evolving.

Incentives and rewards

In nurturing a knowledge culture, an organisation must have rewards and incentive systems in place. Such measures are necessary to motivate knowledge sharing and reward knowledge contribution. Hauschild, Licht and Stein (2001: 76) found that 'less successful companies tend to take a top-down approach: pushing knowledge to where it is needed. Successful companies, by contrast, reward employees for seeking, sharing, and creating knowledge.' Davenport et al. (1998) argue that motivation to contribute knowledge is an intangible critical success factor for any KM project.

However, motivation is a typically difficult issue to address as it relates to changing people's perception and behaviour. It is closely tied to the cultural norm of an organisation. Currently, this issue isn't well addressed. This is reflected in the current KM practice where less management attention is paid to rewards and incentives for knowledge sharing than to employee training, KM systems development, organisational structure and organisational culture (Zhou and Fink, 2003b).

Rewards could be monetary or non-monetary, formal or informal, and long term or short term. Which one(s) to use will depend on the circumstances and requires careful consideration. Formal, monetary rewards such as bonuses, compensation and promotions are not necessarily more powerful than informal, non-monetary rewards. Bonuses, compensation and promotions used to be part of the formal rewards system in organisations but they do not work well in every circumstance. Contrary to what may be expected, inappropriate use of such incentives could discourage knowledge sharing and lead to other counterproductive practices (Hauschild, Licht and Stein, 2001). Tying annual bonuses solely to frontline employees' sales volume, for example, may spark unhealthy competition. Moreover, the growth of sales volume in the short term may be achieved at the expense of customer satisfaction, which can be harmful to the future prospect of the firm.

Non-financial rewards, such as recognition of expertise (e.g. a title of subject matter expert (SME)), extra days' leave, a thank-you note or e-mail, an opportunity for training or a present, can have the same effect as financial rewards. Other incentive measures include coveted office space, an opportunity to travel or to receive more challenging assignments (Hauschild, Licht and Stein, 2001).

Incentives can be long term or short term. If organisations choose short-term incentives, they should be, in the opinion of Davenport et al. (1998), highly visible to attract good public attention. See how Buckman Laboratories did this skilfully in Case study 3.4 below. However, given the fact that people tend to hide knowledge for their own advantage, organisations should focus on long-term motivational approaches, and make the extent of knowledge contribution part of the evaluation and compensation structure (Davenport et al., 1998).

Case study 3.4

Buckman Laboratories

Buckman Laboratories has invested heavily in its knowledge sharing and management system – K'Netix – and strongly believes that incentives can help make the difference between success and failure. To make its online knowledge-sharing networks and knowledge repositories successful, the company offers very visible incentives for those who demonstrate a commitment to knowledge sharing.

To encourage more knowledge sharing behaviour, the company organised a high-profile event in Scottsdale, Arizona at a fashionable resort as a celebration to recognise the 150 best 'knowledge sharers', selected by a panel comprising Buckman's knowledge managers and knowledge network facilitators. These 150 best 'knowledge sharers' were rewarded with a laptop computer, an IBM ThinkPad 755, a leather computer bag, and a presentation by Tom Peters.

The award generated heated discussion among employees, especially those not selected. The event delivered a clear and visible message to all employees that knowledge sharing was recognised and valued by the company, and received an immediate response – participation on the K'Netix forums increased dramatically.

Sources: Davenport et al. (1998) and Rifkin (1996).

When changes need to be made to the established rewards system, an incremental approach would be more workable than a radical one. Rumizen (2002) advises not to make substantial changes as it could cause undesirable effects. When a change is being implemented, employees should be given time to learn and adapt.

Measurement

Historically, the management and measurement of intellectual resources have been pursued separately, and it is the IC perspective that brings these two streams of thought together (see Chapter 6 for more information on the relationship between IC and KM). Managing and measuring can be seen as two sides of the same coin. Organisations cannot effectively manage knowledge without addressing the measurement issue or vice versa. In fact, organisations do not just measure IC for their own sake. There is widespread belief that 'what you can measure you can manage'. The purpose of measurement is to provide metrics and feedback to management, and the outcome of such an exercise should be a more effective knowledge management approach.

In terms of what constitutes IC, although different authors have different views on the aggregated level of IC, IC is generally classified into three sub-categories:

1. *Human capital.* Employee know-how, expertise and experience.

2. *Organisational (internal) capital.* Management, organisational structure, attitudes, R&D, information systems, culture, manuals and procedures and intellectual properties.

3. *Customer (external) capital.* Brands, reputations, customer, supplier and other stakeholder relations.

There are two major schools of thought in approaching the issue of measuring IC. One is the monetary school of thought, rooted in the traditional accounting domain, attempting to extend current accounting practice and apply monetary measure to value IC (e.g. human resource costing and accounting (HRCA) and the technology broker). Another is the holistic school of thought, motivated by the desire for a more holistic and balanced view on performance by adopting both financial and non-financial measures (e.g. the Skandia value scheme and balanced scorecard). These two schools of thought have their advantages and disadvantages, as illustrated in Table 3.1.

Within the monetary school of thought, some models make no attempt to categorise IC. Instead, they measure IC only at an aggregate value at the organisational level. These models can be further divided into two different categories based on the methodology used in calculating the value of intellectual capital. One category adopts what Sveiby (2001) calls the market capitalisation method (MCM) that suggests that the value of intellectual capital is the difference between a firm's market value and the book value of its net assets. This category includes market-to-book value and Tobin's q.

Another category uses the return on assets (ROA) method in which the value of intellectual capital is derived from the excess return on tangible assets by comparing a firm's ROA and the industry average ROA. This category includes Economic Value Added (EVA™), human resource costing and accounting (HRCA), calculated intangible value (CIV), knowledge capital earnings (KCE) and the Value Added Intellectual Coefficient (VAIC™).

Other models within the monetary school of thought use what Sveiby (2001) terms the direct intellectual capital (DIC) method. DIC attempts to evaluate the various components of intangible assets by offering a dollar valuation once they have been identified. Models adopting this methodology include the technology broker, citation-weighted patents and the Value Explorer™.

Table 3.1	Comparison of the two schools of thought for measuring IC	
	Advantages	**Disadvantages**
Monetary school of thought	■ Objectivity ■ Easy to understand ■ Useful for communication and comparison ■ Easier to get attention of CEOs ■ Builds on the strength of accounting	■ May be superficial ■ Subject to manipulation ■ Limited use for internal management purposes ■ Not suitable for non-profit and public sector organisations
Holistic school of thought	■ More comprehensive picture of a firm's health ■ Focuses on a firm's future potential ■ Easily applied at any level of an organisation (also at national level) ■ Faster and more accurate than pure financial measures ■ Useful for non-profit organisations, internal departments and public sector organisations	■ Indicators are contextually specified ■ Difficult to make comparison ■ Not widely accepted ■ Abundant data generated ■ Hard to analyse and communicate

Within the holistic school of thought, all existing models use the scorecard (SC) method. The SC method is similar to the DIC method mentioned above. The only difference is that no attempt is made to estimate IC in monetary terms in the SC approach. After various components of intellectual capital have been identified, indicators and indices under each component can be developed and reported for internal management and external reporting purposes. This category includes the Skandia Navigator™, the IC-Index™, the intangible assets monitor and the balanced scorecard method.

The strengths and weaknesses of each methodology are illustrated in Table 3.2.

The case studies which follow demonstrate how two leading companies, McKinsey and Skandia, implemented measurement models in practice.

Table 3.2 Illustration of the strengths and weaknesses of the four methodologies in measuring IC

School of thought	Methodology	Example	Brief description	Strengths	Weaknesses
Monetary	**MCM:** Market-to-book value (Stewart, 1997); Tobin's q (Stewart, 1997; Bontis, 2001)	Tobin's q	'q' is the ratio of the market value of the firm (share price times number of shares) to its replacement cost (i.e. the cost of replacing its assets). Hence, the larger the 'q' figure, the greater the value of IC	1. Straightforward and easy to understand 2. Easy to calculate	1. Provides an aggregated figure only; does not provide information on individual IC performance 2. Cannot accurately reflect the value of IC in an organisation: 'q' is only a proxy for measuring effective performance 3. May not be applicable to companies that are not listed on the stock market as the market value of those firms is difficult to determine

| Monetary | ROA: EVA™ (Stewart, 1997); HRCA (Sackmann, Flamholz and Bullen, 1989); CIV (Stewart, 1997; Luthy, 1998); KCE (Lev and Mintz, 1999); VAIC™ (Pulic, 2000) | Economic Value Added (EVA™) | EVA™ = Net Sales – Operating Expenses – Taxes – Capital Charges By adjusting a firm's profit with charges related to intangibles imposed by traditional accounting practice, EVA™ is regarded as a surrogate measure for the stock of IC based on the assumption that effective management of knowledge assets increases EVA™. Hence, changes in EVA™ signal the performance of IC | 1. EVA™ is a surrogate measure for the stock of IC and can be viewed as a measure for return on IC 2. Comprehensive performance adjustments, covering up to 164 different areas, solve the traditional accounting problems on intangibles and long-term investments | 1. No specific measures are developed to assess the contribution of individual IC 2. The use of book asset values relies on historical costs, rather than market or replacement value 3. No conclusive evidence on the use of EVA as a better predictor of stock price exists 4. It assumes that companies are run in the interest of shareholders exclusively |

Table 3.2 (continued)

School of thought	Methodology	Example	Brief description	Strengths	Weaknesses
Monetary	**DIC:** Technology broker (Brooking, 1996); CWP (Bontis, 2001); The Value Explorer™ (Andriessen and Tiessen, 2000)	Technology broker	The model assesses the IC value of a firm based on a diagnostic analysis of the firm's response to 20 questions that cover the four major components of IC and make up the IC indicator. The four IC components are identified as 1. market assets 2. human-centred assets 3. intellectual property assets	1. Provides a roadmap for organisations to identify, value and leverage IC 2. Offers a toolbox for organisations to assign value to IC	The main weaknesses of this method relate to its value calculation approaches. Technology broker offers three methods of calculating a dollar value for the IC identified in the auditing processes: 1. *The cost approach*, which uses the replacement cost of the asset. However, a considerable leap has to be made from the qualitative results of the questionnaire to actual dollar values for the asset

2. *The market approach*, which uses comparable market value to assess the value of the asset. However, it is difficult to get accurate or market-based prices for many components of IC

3. *The income approach*, which uses the income-earning capability of the asset (i.e. net present value). However, this approach is influenced by accounting procedures and the uncertainties of cash flow projection

4. infrastructure assets

Each component of IC is audited using a number of questionnaires, and a dollar value of the IC is then calculated upon completion of the audit

Table 3.2 (continued)

School of thought	Methodology	Example	Brief description	Strengths	Weaknesses
Holistic	**SC:** Skandia Navigator™ (Edvinsson, 1997); IC-Index™ (Roos et al., 1997); Intangible assets monitor (Sveiby, 1997); Balanced scorecard (Kaplan and Norton, 1996)	Balanced scorecard	Three non-financial perspectives – customer perspective, internal process perspective, and learning and growth perspective – plus the accounting-based financial perspective. Key success factors (KSF) for each perspective can be developed to meet a firm's strategic objective and translated into a number of critical indicators	1. Widely used in practice 2. A systematic way to measuring different dimensions of performance 3. A sophisticated measurement and management system	1. The design of a scorecard is relatively rigid. The selection of key success factors might be problematic as some are cross-perspective. Moreover, the four perspectives themselves might be limiting 2. The external perspective is limited to customers only. Relationships with suppliers, partners, etc. are not taken into account 3. Employees are treated as an afterthought and knowledge is reified, i.e. it is treated like a concrete, tangible thing 4. It cannot be used for external comparison

Case study 3.5

McKinsey and Skandia

At McKinsey, electronic networks containing the institutional knowledge garnered from past projects play a key role in the fundamental transformation of the company's professional practice and culture.

The company's 30 'practice centres', which are primarily industry-focused, are staffed voluntarily by a virtual community of consultants who aggressively market their expertise to the rest of the company. The objective of maintaining these electronic communities, according to Brook Manville, former director of knowledge management, is to create a dynamic internal marketplace for knowledge exchange. Most of the centres measure how frequently their internal customers use the material contained on the system.

The Organisation Performance Practice Centre is perhaps the most advanced in this regard. With about 70 members, making it one of McKinsey's largest and most active centres, it runs a Rapid Response Network, promising internal customers around the world a quick response to any query. Each Centre consultant acts as an *on-call consultant* at some time during the year, guaranteeing a response within 24 hours to queries from any of 58 offices in 28 countries. The Rapid Response Network performs extensive follow-up and tracks customer satisfaction, publishing an annual report with statistics detailing the Centre's activities.

Skandia takes a much broader and comprehensive approach in measuring and reporting its IC through the Skandia Value Scheme and the Skandia Navigator. Its finance department works with each subsidiary company to develop a set of performance measures tailored to each company's specific situation.

All companies develop measures in these five areas:

- Financial
- Customer
- Human
- Process
- Renewal and development

The set of measures is called a 'Navigator', and companies use it to monitor how well they are managing the critical attributes of intellectual capital.

For example, to help assess Skandia's performance in developing its intellectual capital, non-financial measures are employed. These include:

- the number of ideas customers bring to the company and how they are developed;

- the number of software packages compared to the number of employees;
- how many people are tied into the Internet system;
- how much networking is done between customers and employees;
- the number of good ideas produced;
- the level of education or training for company employees;
- how many good ideas are exchanged between two key departments;
- turnover and retention figures;
- the number of patents granted or articles published.

Having developed a set of non-financial metrics, Skandia takes a step further, working to link those metrics to value expressed in financial terms. It might still be some years away from being able to establish such an economic linkage. Nonetheless, Skandia has started its journey that it believes will lead it closer to this goal of measurably increasing its knowledge base. Activities upon which Skandia embarks include:

- more shareholder-friendly reporting of the company's hidden intellectual resources;
- more refined and broadened financial management control;
- defining the intellectual capital controller role and how it pertains to intellectual capital;
- more systematic comparisons such as benchmarking;
- obtaining cooperation between the accounting and human resources functions to develop indicators and capital ratios that pertain to human capital such as empowerment studies and competency analyses;
- promoting leadership development, management recruitment and leadership values for renewal and development of the group's intellectual capital;
- envisioning the 'secretarial' role in the modern IT-intensive network organisation;
- employing job rotation, or alternatively specialist careers, for better utilisation of the employee's capability for renewal and development;
- utilising systems for the creation of structural capital through IT and the exchange of competencies from a global, corporate perspective.

Sources: Edvinsson (1997), Rosenblum and Keller (1994) and Supplement to Skandia's Annual Report (1994).

Conclusion

This chapter examines the roles of organisational culture, leadership, structure, incentives and rewards, and measurement in KM.

An innovative and entrepreneurial culture has the vision and leadership that focuses on learning, values knowledge, engenders trust and communication, and tolerates questioning and mistakes. A team-based, flat, networked organisational structure encourages communication and collaboration. Leadership plays a critical role in implementing the cultural, organisational and technical change required by KM initiatives, while measurement issues involve developing measures to assess and/or value knowledge resources and processes. Above all, appropriate incentives and rewards are necessary to motivate effective knowledge-sharing behaviour.

Without doubt, an appreciation of the importance of these organisational factors will aid explicit and deliberate efforts in managing knowledge for the desired outcomes.

References

Andriessen, D. and Tiessen, R. (2000) *Weightless Weight: Find Your Real Value in a Future of Intangible Assets.* London: Financial Times Prentice Hall.

Bontis, N. (2001) 'Assessing knowledge assets: a review of the models used to measure intellectual capital', *International Journal of Management Reviews,* 3 (1): 41–60.

Brooking, A. (1996) *Intellectual Capital: Core Assets for the Third Millennium Enterprise.* London: Thomson Business Press.

Chase, R.L. (1997) 'The knowledge-based organisation: an international survey', *Journal of Knowledge Management,* 1 (1): 38–49.

Davenport, T.H. (1996) 'Knowledge roles: the CKO and beyond', *CIO Magazine,* 1 April.

Davenport, T.H., De Long, D.W. and Beers, M.C. (1998) 'Successful knowledge management projects', *Sloan Management Review,* Winter: 43–57.

Edvinsson, L. (1997) 'Developing intellectual capital at Skandia', *Long Range Planning*, 30 (3): 366–73.

Elliott, S. and O'Dell, C. (1999) 'Sharing knowledge and best practices: the how and whys of tapping your organisation's hidden reservoirs of knowledge', *Health Forum Journal*, 42 (3): 34–7.

Essex, D. (2003) 'Knowledge management programs pay big dividends', *ITworld.com*. Available at: *www.itworld.com/App/236/ITW1795/* (accessed 8 October 2003).

Hauschild, S., Licht, T. and Stein, W. (2001) 'Creating a knowledge culture', *McKinsey Quarterly*, 1: 74–81.

Holsapple, C.W. (2003) *Knowledge Management Handbook*. Berlin: Springer.

Imperato, G. (1997) 'Harley shifts gears', *Fast Company*, June/July: 104.

Junnarkar, B. and Brown, C.V. (1997) 'Re-assessing the enabling role of IT in knowledge management', *Journal of Knowledge Management*, 1 (2): 142–8.

Kaplan, R.S. and Norton, D.P. (1996) *The Balanced Scorecard: Translating Strategy into Action*. Boston: Harvard Business School Press.

Knights, D. (1995) 'Refocussing the case study: the politics of research and researching politics in IT management', *Technology Studies*, 2 (2): 230–84.

Leidner, D.E. (1999) 'Information technology and organisational culture', in R.D. Galliers, D.E. Leidner and B.S.H. Baker (eds), *Strategic Information Management: Challenges and Strategies in Managing Information Systems*, 2nd edn. Oxford: Butterworth-Heinemann, pp. 523–50.

Leonard-Barton, D. (1995) *Wellsprings of Knowledge*. Boston: Harvard Business School Press.

Lesser, E.L. and Storck, J. (2001) 'Communities of practice and organisational performance', *IBM Systems Journal*, 40 (4): 831–41.

Lev, B. and Mintz, S.L. (1999) 'Seeing is believing – a better approach to estimating knowledge capital', *CFO Magazine*, February: 29–37.

Lusch, R.F. and Harvey, M.G. (1994) 'The case for an off-balance-sheet controller', *Sloan Management Review*, Winter: 101–5.

Luthy, D.H. (1998) *Intellectual Capital and its Measurement*. Available at: *http://www3.bus.osaka-cu.ac.jp/apira98/archives/htmls/25.htm* (accessed 20 October 2004).

McKeen, J.D. and Staples, D.S. (2000) 'Knowledge managers: who they are and what they do', in C.W. Holsapple (ed.), *Handbook on Knowledge Management*. Berlin: Springer.

Pulic, A. (2000) 'VAIC – an accounting tool for IC management', *International Journal of Technology Management*, 20: 702–14.

Rifkin, G. (1996) 'Buckman Labs is nothing but Net', *Fast Company*, 3, June/July: 118. Available at: *http://www.fastcompany.com/online/03/buckman.html* (accessed 1 November 2004).

Roos, J., Roos, G., Dragonetti, N.C. and Edvinsson, L. (1997) *Intellectual Capital: Navigating the New Business Landscape.* London: Macmillan Business.

Rosenblum, J. and Keller, R. (1994) 'Building a learning organisation at Coopers and Lybrand', *Planning Review*, September–October.

Rumizen, M.C. (2002) *The Complete Idiot's Guide to Knowledge Management.* Madison, WI: CWL Publishing Enterprises.

Sackmann, S., Flamholz, E. and Bullen, M. (1989) 'Human resource accounting: a state of the art review', *Journal of Accounting Literature*, 8: 235–64.

Sharratt, M. and Usoro, A. (2003) 'Understanding knowledge-sharing in online communities of practice', *Electronic Journal of Knowledge Management*, 1 (2): 187–96.

Stewart, T.A. (1997) *Intellectual Capital: The New Wealth of Organisations.* New York: Doubleday.

Supplement to Skandia's Annual Report (1994) *Visualising Intellectual Capital in Skandia.* Available at: *http://www.skandia.com* (accessed 20 October 2004).

Sveiby, K.-E. (1997) *The New Organizational Wealth: Managing and Measuring Knowledge Based Assets.* San Francisco: Berrett-Koehler.

Ward, L.B. (1996) 'In the executive alphabet, you call them C.L.O.'s'. *New York Times*, 4 February.

Wiig, K.M. (1999) *Successful Knowledge Management: Does It Exist?* Available at: *http://www.krii.com* (accessed 15 March 2000).

Zhou, A. and Fink, D. (2003a) 'The intellectual capital web: a systematic linking of intellectual capital and knowledge management', *Journal of Intellectual Capital*, 4 (1): 34–48.

Zhou, A. and Fink, D. (2003b) 'Knowledge management and intellectual capital: an empirical examination of current practice in Australia', *Knowledge Management Research and Practice*, 1 (2): 86–94.

4

The role of technology in KM

Introduction

The role of technology in KM is not well understood. For some time, many organisations considered KM mainly as an IT issue, and adopted a techno-centric or technocratic approach (Zhou and Fink, 2003a). This has led to undesired outcomes in KM implementations. In recent years, organisations that learnt the hard lessons started realising that KM is not only related to technology. It must include other aspects, such as integration of organisational structure, culture and strategic objectives in a systematic approach (Standards Australia, 2001; Zhou and Fink, 2003a).

On the other hand, the view that technology is incidental to KM may also be dangerous. Researchers predict that technology will continue to change the nature of knowledge creation, publication and sharing, and this will have enormous social and managerial implications (Holsapple, 2003). Thus, organisations that ignore or minimise the role of technology in the conduct of KM may lose the chance of success. However, it is important to have a realistic expectation of what IT can and cannot do.

In this book, we take an integrated view of KM and consider KM as a socio-technological phenomenon. The Handzic (2004) KM framework presented in Chapter 1 views KM solutions as configurations of knowledge stocks, processes and enablers. This framework proposes two classes of knowledge enablers: the organisational environment including the organisational culture, organisational structure, leadership and measurement (addressed in Chapter 3) and the technological infrastructure including a wide range of information and communication technologies. This latter knowledge enabler is the focus of this chapter.

The chapter begins by arguing that IT does matter in KM. Then it describes the most common IT solutions currently in use to support the capture, creation and sharing of knowledge assets, e.g. locating useful knowledge, transferring best practice, connecting people with relevant interests and supporting intelligent problem-solving. Finally, taking the contingent view of KM that claims that no one approach is best under all circumstances, the chapter proposes a way to select an appropriate technology to support an organisation's knowledge management effort.

Does IT matter in KM?

In May 2003, Carr (2004) triggered a heated debate around the world over the role of IT in business by writing a *Harvard Business Review* article entitled 'IT Doesn't Matter'. In his recent book called *Does IT Matter?*, Carr (2004) expands on the topic and challenges the commonly held assumptions that IT is increasingly critical to competitive advantage and strategic success. He argues that IT's strategic importance is actually diminishing as any innovations in hardware, software and networking will be quickly copied by competitors.

Central to Carr's argument is the distinction between infrastructural and proprietary technologies, and the proposition that IT has been transformed from a proprietary technology that can be owned by a single company to gain a competitive advantage into an infrastructural technology that is accessible to all (Carr, 2004). Carr's view touches the nerve of anyone who has a stake in IT. Certainly, not everyone will agree to his position. Indeed, no serious players in the market will turn a blind eye to the potential impact that emerging technologies may have on business processes.

While the debate over the role of IT will continue, many would agree that it is probably not IT itself, but the firm's ability to creatively use IT for competitive advantage that matters most. There is ample evidence showing both tangible benefits (e.g. efficiency, cost reductions) and intangible benefits (e.g. improved coordination) brought by the use of IT as a business process enabler. From teleconferencing to virtual teaming, from e-mail to e-commerce, people in different geographical locations can now work on the same project and services can be delivered online 24/7. All these are only made possible through the use of IT.

The innovative use of IT calls for continuous improvement in employee skills and knowledge, a key strategic resource for competitive advantage in the twenty-first century – one of the major theses being argued throughout this book. In this regard, IT helps employees to capture, share and utilise skills and experience. IT plays a significant role in knowledge representation, repositories and transformation, and improves people's ability to acquire and share knowledge (Zhou and Fink, 2003a). An IT infrastructure provides a network platform for the collection, communication and analysis of information and knowledge where the infrastructure serves to help members of an organisation share and transfer knowledge (Davis, 1998). In short, IT has the potential to facilitate the four KM processes of creation, storage/retrieval, transfer and application (Alavi and Leidner, 2001).

Having said that, we do not suggest that 'KM = IT' or that the success of KM primarily depends on IT. Making such a suggestion would be out of proportion to the appropriateness of the role of IT. We must point out that knowledge management does not start or end with IT systems. Moreover, the use of IT is not without its shortcomings and critics. Although some studies have shown that virtual interaction mediated by IT is no less effective than the face-to-face mode of interaction (Warkentin, Sayeed and Hightower, 1997), and, in some cases, is even an effective extension of face-to-face conversation (Sharratt and Usoro, 2003), many people are still sceptical of the facilitating role of IT in knowledge transfer.

Whereas proponents of IT argue that communication mediated by IT provides not only a quick way to receive help and valuable information, but also better access to knowledge from a large pool of people (Wasko and Faraj, 2000), critics warn that such communication lacks the richness of face-to-face conversation (Sharratt and Usoro, 2003) and is incapable of fully developing relationships and understanding of complex situations (Bender and Fish, 2000). Fahey and Prusak (1998) added that 'IT ... can never substitute for the rich interactivity, communication, and learning that is inherent in dialogue' (p. 273). They consider substituting technological contact for human interface being among 'the eleven deadliest sins of KM'.

As mentioned in the last chapter, some organisations recognise the limitations of IT and try to compensate by creating a supportive physical environment to encourage face-to-face contact between employees. Other organisations frequently send out their employees to attend seminars and visit their clients. They also run training courses and workshops for their employees and clients. This helps develop personal relationships and social networks within the organisation and between employees and clients, something valuable to business that cannot be delivered through technology alone. That's why Bender and Fish (2000) argue for the need for multinational firms to employ global assignments involving transferring staff across national boundaries for the transfer of knowledge and the retention of expertise even though most of these firms have sophisticated information systems in place.

Is virtual meeting through videoconferencing a substitute for face-to-face meeting?

For BP Exploration – a division of the global oil giant – the answer is yes. Videoconferencing is used to solve real business problems by facilitating the exchange of tacit knowledge. When a compressor in an oil field in Colombia, South America, ran into trouble, experts on the North Slope of Alaska and in Italy were brought to the scene, through videoconferencing, to help fix the problem in just a few hours.

On the contrary, Chaparral Steel, internationally renowned for its quality and performance, takes a very different approach. To ensure that it remains abreast of the latest industry trends and thinking, the firm regularly sends employees on sabbaticals to visit academic institutions and industry leaders in order to collect best practices and learn about new technologies.

To develop its 'near net-shape' steel beams – large structural steel I-beams costing the same per pound as simple round reinforcing bars – Chaparral sent key employees to Japan, Germany, Italy and Mexico to discover which companies had the equipment that Chaparral would need to accomplish its goal. Based on these visits, Chaparral was able to acquire devices such as the mould used in the steel-making process and the ideas for building a world-class production laboratory for testing.

Chaparral considers the money spent on employee travel to be an investment in learning that pays for itself. Mixed employee teams, which may include foremen, technical staff, vice presidents and operators, visit customers, competitors and suppliers throughout the world. In many cases, newly acquired knowledge does not even have to be filtered down because the employee who gathered it is often the one who will apply it.

Sources: Davenport, De Long and Beers (1998), Garvin (1993) and Leonard-Barton (1995).

All in all, KM system implementations are only part of the process toward a smarter organisation and not a goal in itself. KM will not work without addressing the real business needs and integrating with other work processes (Zhou and Fink, 2003a).

Empirical findings on the role of IT in KM

The findings of a survey of Australian organisations showed that IT was perceived to be less important than organisational culture and organisational structure in facilitating the processes of knowledge creation and sharing.

In terms of which tools are more effective in KM, a number of international and local surveys all point to three technologies – e-mail systems, intranets and the Internet – as the three most effective tools used in managing knowledge (Chase, 1997; Parlby, 2000; Zhou and Fink, 2003b).

It appeared that IT in itself is not a strong enabling tool in KM processes. As Massey et al. (2002: 285) rightly point out, 'In and of itself, technology is not likely sufficient for effective KM.' It seems that KM technical solutions alone offer very moderate effect and might make only a limited contribution to overall KM success.

Source: Zhou and Fink (2003b).

Typology of KM technologies

To help better understand the various roles of IT in KM, the authors have developed a typology of KM technologies. The typology is based on the distinction of KM processes and is used to frame our discussion about the role of IT in these processes. We have made no attempt to exhaustively categorise all IT tools that may potentially be used to support KM.

There are seven categories in the typology (see Table 4.1). Many technologies currently in use that facilitate and support KM can be classified into one of the seven categories based on what knowledge process it supports and what objective it aims to achieve.

- *Knowledge storage technologies* are tools used in the knowledge storage process to capture and store organisational knowledge, with the objective to enhance organisational memory (Alavi and Leidner, 2001) and to provide broader access to knowledge resources (Grover and Davenport, 2001).

- *Knowledge search/retrieval technologies* are tools used in the knowledge retrieval process to locate internal knowledge on intranets or external knowledge on the Internet, with the objective of increasing the speed and accuracy of knowledge search.

- *Knowledge delivery/sharing technologies* are tools used in the knowledge transfer process to distribute knowledge to locations where it is needed and can be applied (Alavi and Leidner, 2001), with the objective of delivering the right knowledge to the right person at the right time.

- *Knowledge discovery and visualisation technologies* are tools used in the knowledge creation process to analyse raw data, with the objective of identifying or uncovering hidden patterns and extracting new knowledge.

- *Knowledge utilisation technologies* are tools used in the knowledge application process to embed knowledge into work processes, with the objective of facilitating knowledge integration and application (Alavi and Leidner, 2001).

- *Platform technologies* are net-based tools that can be used conjointly with other technologies in any KM process to provide a network platform for knowledge collection, communication and analysis (Alavi and Leidner, 2001; Davis, 1998). These networked technologies are

Table 4.1　A typology of KM technologies

Category	KM process	Purpose	Examples
Knowledge storage technologies	Knowledge storage	To store organisational knowledge and enhance organisational memory	Knowledge repositories, databases, text-bases, data warehouse, data marts
Knowledge access technologies	Knowledge storage	To improve access to knowledge and/or facilitate knowledge transfer among individuals	Knowledge maps, knowledge directories, yellow pages
Knowledge search/retrieval technologies	Knowledge retrieval	To locate internal/external knowledge and to improve access to knowledge resources	Search engines, intelligent agents
Knowledge delivery/sharing technologies	Knowledge transfer	To deliver the right knowledge to the right person at the right time	E-mail systems, electronic bulletin boards, whiteboards, electronic forums, videoconferencing, voice mail, groupware
Knowledge discovery and visualisation technologies	Knowledge creation	To uncover hidden patterns and extract new knowledge	Data mining, statistical tools, graphical representation, simulation technologies
Knowledge utilisation technologies	Knowledge application	To facilitate knowledge integration and application	KM systems, workflow systems, expert systems, rule induction, decision trees
Platform technologies	All	Multiple purposes: can be used to support any or all of the above processes	Internet, intranets, extranets, portals

commonly used by organisations to construct a single point of access (e.g. a corporate portal) to multiple sources of knowledge (Grover and Davenport, 2001).

■ *Knowledge access technologies* are tools that can be used to improve access to knowledge stored in knowledge repositories and/or facilitate knowledge transfer among individuals.

While the seven types of KM technologies are discussed separately, it should be noted that they are not mutually exclusive. First, some technologies may be used to support multiple processes and may, therefore, have multiple purposes (e.g. electronic discussion forum). Second, these technologies do not work in isolation. In fact, quite often technologies are combined to produce a synergic effect (e.g. the combination of a knowledge repository and knowledge map). Furthermore, there may be situations where a technology does not fall neatly into any of these seven categories.

There are other classifications of IT tools for KM. Tsui (2003) offered a good overview of the commercial KM software available on the market. Based on functions and techniques, Tsui suggested a framework of KM tools including nine categories – search, meta/web crawler, process modelling and mind mapping, case-based reasoning, data and text mining, taxonomy/ontological tools, groupware, measurement and reporting, and e-learning. Binney (2001) developed a KM spectrum that consists of six categories: transactional, analytical, asset management, process based, developmental and innovation/creation.

For more details on Binney's KM spectrum see the box below.

The KM Spectrum

Binney (2001), based on his experience in working with executives and strategists, developed the KM spectrum with two objectives: as a framework that can assist organisations in better understanding the KM phenomenon, and as a KM assessment and strategic planning tool. A wide range of KM applications and enabling technologies can be mapped into each of the six categories in the spectrum (see Table 4.2).

Table 4.2 The KM spectrum with KM applications and enabling technologies

	Transactional	Analytical	Asset management	Process	Developmental	Innovation and creation
Key characteristics	Knowledge embedded in the application of technology	Deriving trends and patterns from large amount of data or information	Involving codified explicit knowledge and intellectual property (IP)	Best practice and benchmarking	Competencies or capabilities development	Team and/or collaborative environment for knowledge creation
KM applications	*Examples:* Case-based reasoning Help desk applications Customer service applications	Data warehousing Data mining Business intelligence Customer relationship management	IP Knowledge repositories Content management Knowledge valuation	Benchmarking Best practice Process improvement Lessons learned	Skills development Staff competencies Training	Communities Collaboration Discussion groups
Enabling technologies	*Examples:* Expert systems	Intelligent agents	Search engines	Workflow management	Computer-based training	E-mail

Table 4.2 (continued)

Transactional	Analytical	Asset management	Process	Developmental	Innovation and creation
Probability networks	Web crawlers	Knowledge maps	Process modelling tools	Online training	Video conferencing
Rule induction, decision trees	Data analysis and reporting tools				Search engine
					Bulletin boards
					Portals, Internet, intranets, extra-nets

Source: Binney (2001).

Application of IT for KM

Handzic (2004) distinguishes between four roles of technology in supporting knowledge processes: (1) building knowledge repositories; (2) promoting virtual socialisation and collaboration; (3) facilitating knowledge search and discovery; and (4) stimulating creativity and complex problem-solving. Categories 1 and 3 support 'codification', and categories 2 and 4 'personalisation' strategies.

In order to better understand and appreciate the various roles of technology in KM, the discussion below has been arranged in thematic categories based on Handzic (2004) and Tsui (2003).

Creating and improving organisational memory

Creating knowledge repositories is by far the most common type of KM initiative, with the substantial use of knowledge storage technologies, such as databases and textbases. The purpose of employing such a document-centred or codification approach is to enhance organisational memory and provide broader access to knowledge resources.

Knowledge contained in a typical knowledge repository is various, including best practice knowledge, knowledge for sales purposes, lessons learned, knowledge around implementation of information systems, competitive intelligence and 'learning histories' (Grover and Davenport, 2001). Such knowledge is usually embedded in various types of documents (e.g. memos, reports, guidelines and manuals), and can be retrieved easily in a repository.

Electronic data generated by daily transactions are typically stored in structured database systems and constitute a part of the organisational memory. In addition to data and text, multimedia systems organise and make available to users their knowledge assets in a variety of other representational forms, such as images, audio and video forms.

Unlike organisational databases that typically store current data related to specific business functions, a data warehouse stores data that retains historical and cross-functional perspectives. Data are extracted daily from the business transaction systems and from any other system deemed relevant. Compared to data warehouses, which combine databases across an entire enterprise, data marts are usually smaller and focus on a particular subject or department.

Improving knowledge access

The vast amount of codified knowledge stored in repositories may create an excessive cognitive burden for users, and hence discourage people from reusing it. To improve knowledge access, many organisations employ knowledge-maps (k-maps) and/or yellow pages to help quickly locate important knowledge.

A k-map is a diagrammatic representation of and a navigation aid to explicit and tacit knowledge (Grey, 1999; Kim, Suh and Hwang, 2003), which can visually highlight knowledge and relationships within a business context. Davenport and Prusak (1998) note that a k-map is a guide, not a repository, as it does not contain knowledge itself. However, knowledge will be more readily accessible if a k-map is put in place conjoining with a knowledge repository.

Wexler (2001) considers the conceptual foundation of knowledge mapping as a form of communication. Indeed, k-maps communicate what is important and actionable information in business contexts. They direct users to locate actionable information. They help form a shared mental model of the circumstance and assist in advancing the problem. They provide map users with confidence in dealing with complex and/or unfamiliar situations. Furthermore, effective k-maps identify domain experts and facilitate organisational learning (Eppler, 2003; Wexler, 2001).

K-maps are classified into different categories. One classification scheme groups k-maps into three generic types (Plumley, 2003). These are:

- *procedural maps*: existing knowledge and the sources of knowledge are mapped to a business process, which can be any business process, such as production planning or a new products forecasting process;

- *conceptual maps*: a framework or taxonomy for organising and classifying existing knowledge content;

- *competency maps*: a directory of skills and expertise of individuals within an organisation.

There are other classification schemes like the five-type categories proposed by Eppler (2003) which include knowledge application, knowledge structure, knowledge source, knowledge asset and knowledge development maps. Wexler (2001) also identifies five types of knowledge maps as competency, concept, strategy, causal and cognitive maps.

There are various benefits that an organisation can gain from using k-maps. These include enhanced knowledge visibility, improved understanding and improved decision-making. A k-map facilitates decision-making and problem-solving by showing which type of knowledge to use at what stage and the sources of that knowledge (Plumley, 2003; Wexler, 2001). It produces confidence in users (Wexler, 2001) and advances decision-makers' understanding of situations at hand. Furthermore, the use of k-maps facilitates the generation of ideas for knowledge sharing and leveraging (Plumley, 2003).

Through IT-based knowledge maps, knowledge directories or yellow pages, individuals in an organisation are able to more rapidly locate either the knowledge that has already been captured and stored in the organisational knowledge repositories or people who have the needed knowledge (Alavi and Leidner, 2001; Offsey, 1997). Often, such metadata (knowledge about where the knowledge resides) is more valuable than the original knowledge itself (Offsey, 1997).

Discovering and visualising knowledge

Data mining and knowledge discovery technologies can look for hidden patterns in groups of data to discover previously unknown trends or relationships. These applications often use complex and sophisticated algorithms to discover knowledge. Two main goals of knowledge discovery include description and prediction. Whereas description is concerned with identifying patterns for the purpose of presenting them to the user in an easy-to-understand form, prediction focuses on the patterns being 'mined' for the purpose of predicting future values for the variables in question. In addition to trend and association analysis, clustering and classification, the current research efforts in these areas also include the use of intelligent agents and the application of competitive intelligence (Blanning, 2000). Case study 4.1 below shows how a new class of business intelligence systems is being implemented in a number of Australian organisations.

Visualisation tools are intended to assist people in analysing complex data sets by mapping physical properties to the data. Visualisation can map expertise and links between people across the organisation, as well as identify missing knowledge areas. It involves utilising interactive graphics to present information and support interactions between human beings and the task they are doing (Rao and Sprague, 1998).

Case study 4.1

Predictive information systems

It was recently reported by the *Sydney Morning Herald* that a number of Australian organisations including the Australian Securities and Investments Commission (ASIC), Qantas and Coca-Cola Amatil (CCA) are implementing a new class of business intelligence systems or predictive information systems to help improve efficiency, reduce costs and plan for future requirements. These systems can quickly search through huge quantities of data, looking for broad patterns and making them available to users. Consequently, their use leads to better customer service and financial return.

In ASIC's case, the system, called Scamseek, can separate texts with subtle differences and look for scams. The system has dramatically improved the law enforcement agency's productivity since its implementation in June 2004. With Scamseek's help, investigators at ASIC need to read five documents only to find four scams. In the past, they had to read eighty documents to find one.

Altea Plan, a system used by Qantas to process its yield, pricing and inventory, can keep track of passenger bookings and the prices paid, and manage the airline's schedules. Benefits from the application of the system include a reduction in the time taken to perform a daylight-saving schedule, improved integrity of data and shorter training time for users.

Insurer IAG uses delivery point identifier (DPID) systems which store the latitude and longitude of Australian houses to help identify those houses that may be potentially affected in the event of bush-fires, floods or storms. Once those houses are identified, e-mails or SMS messages can then be sent out to alert customers. Through the help of the software tools, IAG is able to predict its number of claims to within a 10 per cent margin of error.

CCA, the soft drink giant, also works to exploit the sale demand patterns identified from data collected by the system at the point of sale. At the Gold Coast Indy car race in October 2004, the system enabled CCA's call-centre staff to move the products in readiness and also take account of the weather forecast for the weekend. This has resulted in a 20 per cent increase in sales during the promotion period.

Source: Head (2004).

Stimulating creativity

Virtual reality and mind games are two groups of technologies that are focused on fostering creativity and innovative problem-solving. Most systems are designed to stimulate creative thinking based on the principle of association, memory retrieval and the use of analogy and metaphor. In multi-participant settings, it is also assumed that generation of creative ideas will be stimulated through participants' interaction where one idea leads to another and the process builds upon itself.

Virtual reality technology enables an individual to become actively immersed in a simulated environment. It can have a dramatic impact on a number of areas including manufacturing, education and training, medical interventions, military preparedness and entertainment. Virtual reality offers a tool that enables people to learn more easily through experiential exercise rather than through memorising rules.

Facilitating knowledge transfer and sharing

Various applications have been developed to support communities of practice and facilitate person-to-person communication for knowledge sharing. Examples include e-mail, electronic discussion forums, bulletin boards, whiteboards, audio and videoconferencing, many of which are extremely popular and widely used in practice. E-mail, for instance, is commonly used in many organisations and is a primary means of communication for many of us.

Electronic discussion forums are another common feature for many corporate intranets and the Internet. In an electronic discussion forum, people virtually interact with each other in an anywhere-anytime mode. Virtual interaction is one mode of person-to-person interaction. It is an important mechanism for the exchange of knowledge and experience, especially in today's globalised world, enabling people located in different places and time zones to work together. (Case study 4.2 shows how Buckman employees share knowledge through K'Netix.)

Although there are ongoing debates about the role of IT in the process of knowledge transfer, the virtual mode of interaction will inevitably become a major alternative to traditional face-to-face conversation in an increasingly digitalised world. Wasko and Faraj (2000) note that virtual interaction offers additional benefits as compared to face-to-face conversation. It provides not only a quick way to receive help and valuable information, but also better access to knowledge from a large pool of people.

Case study 4.2

K'Netix system

K'Netix is a global knowledge sharing and transfer system created in the early 1990s by Buckman Laboratories, a specialty chemicals manufacturer renowned for being a pioneer of knowledge management. The system, which enables Buckman's employees around the world to access it, is regarded as a pillar of Buckman's innovative culture.

Featured with electronic discussion forums, bulletin boards, virtual conference rooms, libraries and e-mail, the system encourages open and unrestricted communication among subject experts and the free exchange of ideas, making the application of ideas easier. Buckman's sales representatives can log on to the system and get unlimited access to information and resources in more than 90 countries. The customer information centre has a complete file cabinet for each customer, containing all available information about that customer including internal memos, documents and sales orders.

Through K'Netix, which is based on CompuServe's global information services, front-line employees, no matter where they are located, are able to access any of the seven technical forums and work together directly to solve customer problems. The objective is to win business and to serve the customer by deploying knowledge at the point of sale.

For example, to tender for a US$6 million pitch-control program for an Indonesian mill, Buckman's managing director for Asia who is based in Singapore sent out a call via K'Netix for help. He received 11 responses from six countries including Canada, Sweden, Spain, France, South Africa and New Zealand, supplying their own experience and other relevant information in developing a successful strategy for pitch-control.

Buckman Laboratories won the contract.

Sources: Bender and Fish (2000) and Rifkin (1996).

Improving knowledge flow and utilisation

Closely associated with knowledge transfer is the workflow involving the flow of knowledge that allows a number of employees collaborating on one single project and the deployment of that knowledge for intelligent decision-making. Technologies used to facilitate the flow and utilisation of knowledge include groupware, workflow systems and knowledge-based systems (KBS).

Groupware provides common virtual space for people to collaborate (Tsui, 2003). Its common features include e-mail communications, instant messaging, discussion areas, file areas or document repositories, information management tools and a search facility. Groupware allows members of a group working on a report to keep track of the work or rework done by each individual member.

Workflow systems, usually incorporating some sort of document management facility, are designed to route documents from one person to another in a specified sequence and time. It would, for instance, route a sales inquiry to a sales support person who would follow up the process, such as checking the availability of the product or service and status of delivery and payment.

In the context of decision-making, KBS enable knowledge workers to apply the best decision-making expertise and thus to improve business performance (Davenport and Prusak, 1998). In general, KM systems designed for decision support aim to harness KM technologies in ways that facilitate and enhance decision-making processes. Case study 4.3 demonstrates how Nortel Networks utilises IT to improve performance of its new product development (NPD) process.

Case study 4.3

Virtual Mentor

Virtual Mentor is an electronic performance support system (EPSS) used by Nortel Networks to support the diverse needs of its knowledge workers in Nortel's front-end new product development (NPD) process. EPSS is a new paradigm that integrates principles found in areas such as artificial intelligence and human performance technology. An EPSS has its distinctive feature in which performance is enabled in the context of knowledge work.

Virtual Mentor was developed in 1996 and became the key enabler of Nortel's effort to implement their newly designed front-end NPD process, called Galileo. The reason for developing Virtual Mentor was that options involving the support of human expertise to implement the process were considered too costly and difficult to implement effectively. IT that could be leveraged to create an electronic version of a human expert became a favoured alternative.

Essentially, Virtual Mentor automates each stage of the Galileo process, supports the work of three knowledge worker groups, and manages Nortel's intellectual property. For the three knowledge worker groups – idea generators, decision-makers and process owners, Virtual Mentor provides three different forms of performance support:

- *Knowledge-based support to idea generators.* This support is provided on demand through context-specific advice for each question or activity in the first three phases of the Galileo process.

- *Decision-making support to decision-makers.* This support is provided by codifying and structuring concept information for the purpose of evaluation and comparison.

- *Productivity-based support to process owners charged with tracking progress.* This support is provided via a customised interface to the system that automates searches and other tasks.

The implementation of Virtual Mentor was a great success at Nortel. The tool has enabled Nortel to:

1. efficiently leverage multidisciplinary knowledge assets in the NPD front-end process;

2. improve NPD decision-making processes; and

3. facilitate learning and knowledge exchange.

Sources: Massey, Montoya-Weiss and O'Driscoll (2002) and O'Driscoll, Massey and Montoya-Weiss (1999).

KM technologies selection

Having gained a good understanding of what IT can do for us in KM, we next consider how organisations select appropriate IT tools to support KM initiatives.

Given the variety of roles IT plays in KM, it is not surprising that managers find selecting appropriate KM technologies a daunting and tricky task. KM technologies selection involves a number of considerations in terms of aligning knowledge strategy with organisational strategic objectives, deciding on IT strategy and aligning process, people and technology.

The choice of KM technologies must follow an organisation's strategic objectives. These (including present and future objectives) provide guidelines on the organisation's future direction and knowledge strategy formulation (Zhou and Fink, 2003b). Depending on what strategic objective to pursue and the characteristics of work tasks, an organisation may employ different strategies to manage knowledge.

There are two well-known strategies suggested by Hansen, Nohria and Tierney (1999), codification and personalisation. These two strategies differ in the way that computer technologies are used for managing knowledge. In the codification or document-centred strategy, knowledge storage and access technologies, such as knowledge repositories and knowledge-maps, are used extensively to locate, codify, store and deliver knowledge. In contrast, a personalisation or community-based approach uses knowledge delivery technologies, such as whiteboards and video-conferencing, to help communicate and share knowledge, not to store it. The focus is to develop knowledge communities (human networks supported by IT) so that knowledge and experience can be shared through peer-to-peer interaction.

The choice of a knowledge strategy is a matter of pursuing the right balance between personalisation and codification. The emphasis will depend on the focus of the organisation's strategic direction and the nature of its business (Hansen et al., 1999; Zhou and Fink, 2003b). The codification approach works well when there are repeated (or similar) tasks and knowledge can be reapplied and reused. In contrast, the personalisation approach is a preferable choice if work tasks are unique and employees rely on tacit knowledge to solve problems (Tsui, 2003).

Once a knowledge strategy is formulated, the next logical step is to consider an IT strategy. How much do we spend on IT? Do we pursue cutting-edge technologies? Do we implement radical change? Or can we build on existing systems? To respond to the increasing trend of IT commoditisation, Carr (2004) offers four pieces of advice to managers in relation to or upon considering IT investment and management: spend less; follow, don't lead; innovate when risks are low; and focus more on vulnerabilities than opportunities. In planning IT investments, it is important that priorities are established and existing KM activities and IT systems are taken into account.

Operationally, the choice of KM technologies is determined by the business processes and people tasked with process activities. This requires a systematic linking of process, people and technology (Massey et al., 2002; Zhou and Fink, 2003a, 2003b). Unsurprisingly, one will not be able to propose a precise technology specification without having a good knowledge of the processes and people involved. This is clearly demonstrated in the case of Nortel discussed in the subsection above. As Massey et al. (2002) observed, 'by understanding "what to do" (process) and human and knowledge sources (people) first, the Galileo team was able to more precisely specify technology use and requirements' (p. 285). A clearly defined process and a deep understanding of people's need of data, information and knowledge are important factors in specifying the role of technology (Massey et al., 2002). Furthermore, the typology of KM technologies or the KM spectrum described earlier provides a useful framework in mapping a wide range of technologies available to an organisation.

In terms of the choices in the deployment of KMS, Tsui (2003) presents five options for consideration: (1) customised off-the-shelf; (2) in-house development; (3) solution re-engineering; (4) knowledge services; and (5) knowledge marketplace. Each option has its own advantages and disadvantages (see Table 4.3). Hence, organisations may consider adopting a combination of the above options during the design and deployment stages (Tsui, 2003).

Conclusion

In this chapter, we discuss the facilitating roles of IT in the processes of knowledge creation, storage/retrieval, transfer and application.

Advances in IT have fuelled the widespread growth of the KM phenomenon. In particular, the application of net-based technologies (e.g. the Internet, intranets) is transforming and will continue to shape the way that business is done and how we communicate with each other. IT enables us to do what may otherwise be impossible due to the constraints imposed by time and/or geographical factors. The trend in IT development appears to be accelerating and an increased impact of IT in commerce and business can be expected.

At a technological level, it is important that organisations can propose, select and design appropriate technological interventions to support knowledge processes. Managers need to be able to identify and appraise those technological factors that support communication and collaboration activities. Management's decisions on the development of knowledge strategy and the choice of IT tools to support KM will be critical in getting value for money from their IT investment. Here, we risk overstressing the point we have made time and time again throughout this chapter – KM does not begin or end with IT and IS. Instead it represents just one of the many facets of KM implementation. For a more comprehensive study of the role of technology in KM, interested readers are referred to Handzic (2004).

Table 4.3 A comparison of five options for deploying KM systems

	Customised off-the-shelf (COTS)	In-house development	Solution re-engineering	Knowledge services	Knowledge marketplace
Description	Customise off-the-shelf packaged products from KM tool vendors to suit the organisation's own needs	KM systems are developed in-house	With assistance of outside experts, adapt existing and generic solutions to fit the organisation's own needs	KM applications are provided and hosted by a third party on the Web	A website hosted by a third-party that brings many suppliers of knowledge services
Advantages	■ A traditional way of deploying IT ■ May be piloted ■ Customisation	■ Tailor-made ■ Unique	■ Similar to COTS ■ Adapting existing and generic solutions (not packaged product) ■ Customisation	■ One type of outsourcing ■ Like utility service ■ No licensing fee ■ No development or in-house maintenance costs ■ Guaranteed service	■ Third-party vendor host ■ One-stop knowledge services

Table 4.3 (*continued*)

	Customised off-the-shelf (COTS)	In-house development	Solution re-engineering	Knowledge services	Knowledge marketplace
Dis-advantages	■ Overwhelming numbers of tools	■ Potentially high cost ■ Complex ■ Staff skills requirement ■ Timelines	■ May be difficult to get an existing solution that closely matches what is needed	■ No or little customisation ■ Issues of security and privacy	■ New and evolving

Source: Tsui (2003).

References

Alavi, M. and Leidner, D.E. (2001) 'Knowledge management and knowledge management systems: conceptual foundations and research issues', *MIS Quarterly*, 25 (1): 107–36.

Bender, S. and Fish, A. (2000) 'The transfer of knowledge and the retention of expertise: the continuing need for global assignments', *Journal of Knowledge Management*, 4 (2): 125–37.

Binney, D. (2001) 'The knowledge management spectrum: understanding the KM landscape', *Journal of knowledge Management*, 5(1): 33–42.

Blanning, R.W. (2000) *Knowledge Management and Electronic Commerce*. Paper presented at the Position Papers on Future Directions in Decision Support Research, IFIP, WK8.3, Working Conference on DSS, Stochholm, pp. 5–7.

Carr, N.G. (2004) *Does IT Matter? Information Technology and the Corrosion of Competitive Advantage*. Boston: Harvard Business School Press.

Chase, R.L. (1997) 'The knowledge-based organisation: an international survey', *Journal of Knowledge Management*, 1 (1): 38–49.

Davenport, T.H. and Prusak, L. (1998) *Working Knowledge: How Organisations Manage What They Know*, 1st edn. Boston: Harvard Business School Press.

Davenport, T.H., De Long, D.W. and Beers, M.C. (1998) 'Successful knowledge management projects', *Sloan Management Review*, Winter: 43–57.

Davis, M.C. (1998) 'Knowledge management: information strategy', *The Executive's Journal*, Fall: 11–22.

Eppler, M.J. (2003) 'Making knowledge visible through knowledge maps: concepts, elements, cases', in C.W. Holsapple (ed.), *Handbook on Knowledge Management*. New York: Springer, pp. 187–205.

Fahey, L. and Prusak, L. (1998) 'The eleven deadliest sins of knowledge management', *California Management Review*, 40 (3): 265–76.

Garvin, D.A. (1993) 'Building a learning organisation', *Harvard Business Review*, July–August.

Grey, D. (1999) *Knowledge Mapping: A Practical Overview*. Available at: *http://www.smithweaversmith.com/knowledg2.htm* (accessed 22 April 2004).

Grover, V. and Davenport, T.H. (2001) 'General perspectives on knowledge management: fostering a research agenda', *Journal of Management Information System*, 18 (1): 5–21.

Handzic, M. (2004) *Knowledge Management through the Technology Glass*. Singapore: Word Scientific.

Hansen, M.T., Nohria, N. and Tierney, T. (1999) 'What's your strategy for managing knowledge?', *Harvard Business Review*, 77 (2): 106–16.

Head, B. (2004) 'Knowledge is power', *Sydney Morning Herald*, 16 November, p. 5.

Holsapple, C.W. (2003) *Knowledge Management Handbook*. Berlin: Springer.

Kim, S., Suh, E. and Hwang, H. (2003) 'Building the knowledge map: an industrial case study', *Journal of Knowledge Management*, 7 (2): 34–45.

Leonard-Barton, D. (1995) *Wellsprings of Knowledge: Building and Sustaining the Sources of Information*. Boston: Harvard Business School Press.

Massey, A.P., Montoya-Weiss, M.M. and O'Driscoll, T.M. (2002) 'Knowledge management in pursuit of performance: insights from nortel networks', *MIS Quarterly*, 26 (3): 269–89.

O'Driscoll, T.M., Massey, A.P. and Montoya-Weiss, M.M. (1999) *Virtual Mentor: Enabling Knowledge Management through an Electronic Performance Support System*, 1999 SIM International Paper Awards Competition. Available at: *http://www.simnet.org/library/doc/eprfsupp.doc* (accessed 15 August 2003).

Offsey, S. (1997) 'Knowledge management: linking people to knowledge for bottom line results', *Journal of Knowledge Management*, 1 (2): 113–22.

Parlby, D. (2000) *Knowledge Management Research Report 2000*. London: KPMG Consulting.

Plumley, D. (2003) 'Process-based knowledge mapping', *Knowledge Management Magazine*, March.

Rao, R. and Sprague, R.H. (1998) 'Natural technologies for knowledge work: information visualisation and knowledge extraction', *Journal of Knowledge Management*, 2 (2): 70–80.

Rifkin, G. (1996) 'Buckman Labs is nothing but Net', *Fast Company*, 3, June/July: 118. Available at: *http://www.fastcompany.com/online/03/buckman.html* (accessed 1 November 2004).

Sharratt, M. and Usoro, A. (2003) 'Understanding knowledge-sharing in online communities of practice', *Electronic Journal of Knowledge Management*, 1 (2): 187–96.

Standards Australia (2001) *Knowledge Management: A Framework for Succeeding in the Knowledge Era*. Sydney.

Tsui, E. (2003) 'Tracking the role and evolution of commercial knowledge management software', in C.W. Holsapple (ed.), *Handbook on Knowledge Management*, Vol. 2. New York: Springer, pp. 5–27.

Warkentin, M.E., Sayeed, L. and Hightower, R. (1997) 'Virtual teams versus face-to-face teams: an exploratory study of web-based conference system', *Decision Sciences*, 28 (4): 975–96.

Wasko, M. and Faraj, S. (2000) '"It is what one does": why people participate and help others in electronic communities of practice', *Journal of Strategic Information Systems*, 9: 155–73.

Wexler, M.N. (2001) 'The who, what and why of knowledge mapping', *Journal of Knowledge Management*, 5 (3): 249–63.

Zhou, A. and Fink, D. (2003a) 'The intellectual capital web: a systematic linking of intellectual capital and knowledge management', *Journal of Intellectual Capital*, 4 (1): 34–48.

Zhou, A. and Fink, D. (2003b) 'Knowledge management and intellectual capital: an empirical examination of current practice in Australia', *Knowledge Management Research and Practice*, 1 (2): 86–94.

Knowledge manipulation processes

Introduction

Knowledge management consists of a dynamic and continuous set of processes and practices (Alavi and Leidner, 2001). While a number of classifications of KM processes[1] have been suggested, for the purpose of clarity, we adopt the four generic KM processes suggested by Alavi and Leidner (2001). These are knowledge creation, knowledge storage/retrieval, knowledge sharing/transfer and knowledge application processes.

Knowledge manipulation processes are at the centre of our integrative KM framework presented in Chapter 1. In essence, the development of an organisation's intellectual capital or knowledge assets is the result of the dynamic organisational knowledge processes. The effectiveness of these processes is impacted by a number of organisational and technological factors discussed in the last two chapters.

Managers are responsible for developing and implementing an optimal mix of knowledge processes to support the knowledge needs of an organisation. Hence, it is important that they have a good understanding of the dynamism of these knowledge processes. To this end, in this chapter, we address in turn each of the four processes of knowledge creation, storage/retrieval, transfer and application.

Knowledge creation process

Organisational knowledge creation refers to the process by which new content is developed or replaced within the collective stock of knowledge (Pentland, 1995). Knowledge creation has been one of the major themes in KM research, and one can find a high volume of literature dedicated to the topic. The work of Nonaka and his colleagues is particularly significant and has greatly improved our understanding of how knowledge is created and what conditions support knowledge creation.

Based on the distinctions of tacit–explicit, individual–collective knowledge, Nonaka and Takeuchi (1995) formalise a generic model of organisational knowledge creation – the so-called SECI model – which suggests that new knowledge is the outcome of the continual interplay between tacit and explicit dimensions of knowledge. The SECI model consists of four modes (see Figure 5.1), through which explicit and tacit knowledge are exchanged and transformed:

- *Socialisation* enables tacit knowledge to be shared between individuals. In this process, knowledge is transferred through learning by doing.

- *Externalisation* converts tacit knowledge into explicit knowledge in the form of models, concepts and metaphors.

Figure 5.1   Four processes of knowledge conversion

		To	
		Tacit	**Explicit**
From	**Tacit**	Socialisation	Externalisation
	Explicit	Internalisation	Combination

- *Combination* allows the existing explicit knowledge to be restructured, systemised and combined into new forms of knowledge.

- *Internalisation* enables individuals to absorb explicit knowledge, thus allowing them to broaden their tacit knowledge base so that new knowledge and skills can be developed.

The central theme in these processes is to transform an individual's tacit knowledge into explicit knowledge and make it available to the organisation as a whole. This will then ignite new knowledge and innovative activities (Nonaka and Takeuchi, 1995).

Conditions for knowledge creation

To address the fundamental conditions for knowledge creation, Nonaka and Konno (1998) introduced the concept of 'ba' – a Japanese word which refers to a shared space that serves as a foundation of knowledge creation. According to Nonaka and Konno (1998), 'ba' is an important concept in the theory of knowledge creation because it is a shared space for new knowledge to emerge. Four types of 'ba' corresponding to the four processes of knowledge conversion are described below:

- *'Originating ba'* represents the *socialisation* mode and is the place from which the knowledge creation process begins. Such a common space is needed so that people can share knowledge and experiences through face-to-face conversations.

- *'Interacting ba'* represents the *externalisation* mode and is the place where tacit knowledge is converted into explicit knowledge. In interacting ba, people share knowledge through dialogue and collaboration.

- *'Cyber ba'* represents the *combination* mode and is the virtual place of interaction. In cyber ba, people interact and communicate virtually utilising modern network technologies.

- *'Exercising ba'* represents the *internalisation* mode and is the place where explicit knowledge is converted to tacit knowledge. 'Exercising ba' provides a common space for continuous individual learning and reflection.

To enhance organisational knowledge creation, it is important to understand the characteristics of 'ba' and their relationship with the corresponding mode of knowledge creation (Alavi and Leidner, 2001).

Attention should be paid to the conditions that form part of an organisational environment conducive to knowledge creation. These include, among others, giving people the freedom to have new ideas, giving people time to think, letting people pursue their own projects and providing creative zones spatially separated from the normal working environment. Tolerance for mistakes is also an important factor, as is the congruence of individual interests with the collective goals.

Aids to innovation also include methods for planning and guiding the innovation process. These vary from techniques for stimulating creativity and rewarding employee suggestions to formalising a systematic approach to problem-solving and to using metaphors for expressing tacit knowledge. Stimulating techniques can be classified into three basic categories: free association, structured relationships and group techniques (Marakas, 1999). In the category of structured relationship techniques, the focus is on the generation of new ideas via forced combinations of diverse ideas or concepts. However, the most widely used techniques involve using brainstorming methods in groups to generate ideas. The end result is a map that contains a set of ideas that can be evaluated, organised and prioritised.

How knowledge is developed in organisations

The development of organisational knowledge starts from individuals. Processes that combine the efforts of many individual employees form the core competencies of a company. One of the key factors in the development of organisational knowledge is interaction and communication among individual members. Developing and maintaining relationships and interdependencies among individual employees may be more crucial for organisational success than individual knowledge. Transparency and integration are also important. Knowledge development can be held back or become costly because of unused or unknown experts, or the lack of integration of individual skills into group competencies. Some favourable conditions for successful teamwork are outlined below:

- *Small team size.* This facilitates meetings and communication among team members, encourages open and interactive discussions, enables a better understanding of each other's role and skills, and makes sub-teams possible if more people are necessary to do the required work.

- *Adequate levels of complementary skills.* A combination of technical, problem-solving and interpersonal skills at appropriate levels enables the team to achieve its goals more easily.

- *Meaningful shared purpose.* Articulation of a shared team purpose that constitutes broader and deeper aspirations facilitates communication and mutual understanding between team members.

- *Specific goals.* Specifying clear and measurable team goals, as opposed to organisational or individual goals, helps the team to assess their potential, set priorities, define concrete sets of work products and measure the team's final success.

- *Clear working approach.* A working approach that is concrete, clear and agreed by everybody facilitates the team to achieve its objectives, enables them to better capitalise on existing members' knowledge and further enhances members' skills.

- *Mutual accountability.* Mutual accountability for the team's purpose, goals, approach and work products strengthens the sense of 'only the team can fail', with all members being clear on how they are individually and jointly responsible for the progress and how they are measured against specific goals.

Source: Probst, Raub and Romhardt (2000).

Knowledge storage/retrieval process

Organisational knowledge storage/retrieval involves storing, organising and retrieving organisational knowledge in various forms, such as written documentation, structured information, codified knowledge, documented organisational procedures and processes and tacit knowledge (Alavi and Leidner, 2001; Walsh and Ungson, 1991).

The focus of organisational knowledge storage is to develop and improve organisational memory by building knowledge repositories. Organisational memory is referred to as 'the means by which knowledge from the past experience and events influence present organisational activities' (Stein and Zwass, 1995: 85). Organisational memory may have both positive and negative impacts on behaviour and performance (Alavi and Leidner, 2001). On the one hand, it facilitates change management (Wilkins and Bristow, 1987). It also helps to avoid reinventing the wheel. On the other hand, organisational memory can result in decision-making bias at the individual level and maintaining the status quo at the organisational level.

As mentioned in the last chapter, building knowledge repositories is the commonest type of KM initiative, with the objective of capturing and storing knowledge for later access and reuse (Grover and Davenport, 2001). Markus (2001) identifies three different purposes of building a repository, namely documenting for the document producers themselves, documenting for others with a similar background to the document producers and documenting for others with a dissimilar background to the document producers. Based on the observation that different knowledge reusers need different things from knowledge repositories, Markus suggests that two major factors – who authors the entries and for whom they author the entries – impact the quality and contents of a knowledge repository, which in turn impact the success of subsequent knowledge reuse.

Roles of knowledge repositories in knowledge reuse

1. *Documenting for themselves.* People often produce notes and documents on anything they think might be useful for their own use later. These notes and documents may contain hints for solving certain problems, a rationale for making decisions or points on something of interest. Due to its personal nature, this type of documentation is not aimed for public use, is most likely for short-term use and might not be useful to others.

2. *Documenting for similar others.* This means that the documents will be made publicly available to other people with a similar background who usually have a common context and understanding of what has been produced. Because of this, the task of documenting would not be that burdensome. However, what and how much knowledge to include remains a difficult issue to determine, and might be a very challenging task for the document producers.

3. *Documenting for dissimilar others.* This might be the most difficult and complex process. As documents are knowingly prepared and created for people who are dissimilar to the documenters themselves, the process involves a number of considerations, such as re-authoring the available information and removing contextual information to make it more general, sacrificing accuracy for understandability and withholding sensitive information when needed. To reduce unwillingness to share information, anonymity of records can be utilised. However, this approach has its weakness too – it reduces the ability of knowledge reusers to judge the quality of contributions, which is one of the important factors in the success of knowledge reuse.

Source: Markus (2001).

Conditions for building good knowledge repositories

From the foregoing discussion, it is clear that organisational knowledge storage is not as simple and straightforward a process as some might expect. Like any other information system, if a repository ignores or cannot meet the needs of its users, it will be of little use. To address the issue of how to develop successful knowledge repositories, in addition to the authorship of entries mentioned above, Markus (2001) suggests that careful attention should be paid to three additional factors: the costs involved in creating and using good repository records, how to motivate high quality contributions, and the role of human and technical intermediaries in knowledge documenting and reuse:

- *Providing adequate time and resources.* The task of making good documentation can be very time-consuming and resource-demanding. However, most knowledge workers are busy professionals, and documentation may not be their first priority. The potentially high costs can act as a disincentive for knowledge workers to produce and use quality documentation.

- Hence, appropriate incentives are needed to encourage quality submissions and contributions. These may include explicit reward systems and an open, sharing organisation culture (see Chapter 3).

- Intermediates or facilitators can play an important role in building good knowledge repositories. They abstract, index, author (re-author), translate, synthesise and sanitise a variety of raw materials to create knowledge records for reuse. Markus (2001) observes that much of the documenting work is done most effectively by human intermediaries, and their roles in knowledge reuse are currently under-appreciated. Nonetheless, technology is taking an increasing role in knowledge documenting and reuse (see Chapter 4).

Davenport and Glaser (2002) present an interesting case study in which Partners HealthCare embeds knowledge into the technology that knowledge workers use to do their jobs. The advantage of this approach is that knowledge management becomes part of what people do at work, rather than a separate activity requiring additional time and motivation (see Case study 5.1 below).

Knowledge sharing/transfer process

Organisational knowledge transfer involves distributing knowledge to where it is needed and can be applied (Pentland, 1995). The goal is to distribute the right knowledge to the right people at the right time. The sharing and distribution of knowledge are vital preconditions for turning isolated information or expertise into something that is valuable to the organisation as a whole. Case study 5.1 shows how just-in-time knowledge delivery is implemented at Partners HealthCare.

Case study 5.1

Just-in-time knowledge delivery

It is practically impossible for anyone to keep up with the knowledge being generated in a given profession. People learn, but they also forget. So we often see that mistakes are repeated, lessons learned from others' experience are ignored, and vital information for making effective decisions is not accessible or inadequate. Organisations have been dreaming to have a system that can deliver knowledge when it is needed. A just-in-time knowledge system will deliver just that.

Different from building knowledge repositories or developing communities of practice, a just-in-time knowledge system has the distinctive feature of knowledge embedded in the system so that the right knowledge is readily accessible for knowledge workers to do their jobs. The message is clear: knowledge is useful only when it can be put to use to achieve results.

Partners HealthCare, a Boston-based umbrella organisation, is a pioneer in exploring the potential of a just-in-time knowledge system for their physician order entry. Partners' approach is built on a set of integrated information systems including a patient-record system, a clinical-decision support system, an event-management system and an intranet portal. These all draw from a single knowledge base and use a common logic engine that runs physicians' orders through a series of checks and decision rules. And most importantly, these are all implemented in real time and automatically – the system interacts with the physician and will bring out the knowledge the physician needs immediately without he or she having to seek it out.

Source: Davenport and Glaser (2002).

The channels for knowledge transfer can be informal or formal, personal or impersonal (Alavi and Leidner, 2001; Holtham and Courtney, 1998). Each transfer channel has its own strengths and weaknesses (see Table 5.1). The most effective transfer mechanism depends upon the type of knowledge being transferred (Inkpen and Dikur, 1998). For instance, for highly personal 'tacit' knowledge, contextual case studies and workshops are proposed to be the most effective transfer media, while for easily articulated 'explicit' knowledge, the most effective media include graphs and codified data.

In its commonest form, knowledge transfer takes place through dialogue with colleagues and informal exchanges about how 'things are done around here'. It usually happens during coffee-break conversations or unscheduled meetings and may be effective in promoting socialisation. However, such an approach may preclude the wide dissemination of knowledge. On the other hand, formal mechanisms such as training sessions (on-the-job or classroom) are believed to ensure greater distribution of knowledge but may inhibit creativity. Activities such as seminars and retreats can provide a good opportunity for a company to present its major initiatives and strategies to a wider employee audience. Similarly, professional training and personnel development programmes

Table 5.1   **Comparison between the four channels of knowledge transfer**

Type of channel	Example	Strength	Weakness
Informal transfer	Informal meetings, coffee break conversations	■ Encourage socialisation ■ Effective in small organisations	■ May inhibit greater diffusion
Formal transfer	Training workshops, education programs	■ Effective in wide distribution	■ May hinder creativity
Personal transfer	Apprenticeships, mentoring programs	■ Effective in transferring highly context-specific and situated knowledge	■ May be constrained by time and resource
Impersonal transfer	Knowledge repositories	■ Easy access to knowledge that is readily generalised to other contexts	■ May discourage people from reusing due to the vast amount of knowledge in the repositories

are good methods of spreading knowledge and keeping relevant employees' competencies at a constant high level.

An alternative to the above approaches is impersonal knowledge transfer through, for instance, knowledge repositories. This approach is effective in distributing knowledge that can be readily generalised to different contexts. Today, operational and technical manuals (traditional or computerised) are still an important source of knowledge in many companies. They are used to familiarise employees with rules and regulations pertaining to routine work processes. They can also be a useful way of passing on knowledge about processes proven to be successful (i.e. best practice). Recorded knowledge also supports knowledge preservation. It is much less likely that such knowledge will be lost when someone leaves the company.

Conditions for knowledge transfer

Knowledge transfer is not a simple process, as organisations often do not know what they know and have weak systems for locating and retrieving knowledge that resides within the organisation. Organisations must nurture a supportive organisational environment and establish a technical infrastructure to facilitate knowledge sharing and transfer. These include (1) making knowledge visible; (2) developing knowledge networks; and (3) providing organisational support, most of which have been discussed in Chapters 3 and 4.

1. *Making knowledge visible.* If the existing individual and organisational assets can be visualised, retrieved and located, then the conditions for the sharing and distribution of knowledge are in place. Directories of experts or yellow pages can be used to raise the visibility of specialist knowledge. For example, the directory can list problem areas that occur frequently, together with names of potential problem-solvers. Knowledge maps of various kinds may also be used to locate expertise.

2. *Developing knowledge networks.* For organisations operating on a global scale, computer-supported knowledge networks are useful. The modern technical infrastructure for knowledge distribution includes two main categories of technologies: company-wide data networks such as intranets, and groupware or computer-supported cooperative networks. Intranets offer a high level of security and permit knowledge assets to be used without delay owing to internal

administration. Compared to communication networks (e.g. e-mail), groupware offers extra functionality (e.g. group scheduler) that co-ordinates knowledge distribution and helps to ensure consistency.

3. *Organisational support.* While technical infrastructure is needed for the efficient distribution of knowledge, it is not sufficient to ensure effective knowledge transfer in an organisation. There must also be sufficient willingness among employees to communicate knowledge. At an individual level, this willingness may be influenced by factors such as pride in one's knowledge, availability of time and fear of endangering one's own position. Company culture can also affect the scope and content of knowledge transfer. The use of power, an atmosphere of trust and management attitudes all play a part in creating the right culture for effective knowledge transfer.

Knowledge application process

Organisational knowledge application refers to the process of applying knowledge in practice so that knowledgeable or competent performance can be achieved (Pentland, 1995). Knowledge application is one of the most important aspects of KM as it is where the source of competitive advantage resides (Alavi and Leidner, 2001). The ultimate goal of KM is to utilise knowledge for the benefit of the organisation, and only the productive use of knowledge will translate the accumulated intangible assets into tangible results. Without effective utilisation, all the effort that goes into knowledge development and distribution would be in vain.

There are three primary mechanisms for integrating knowledge to create organisational capability (Alavi and Leidner, 2001; Grant, 1996). These include directives, organisational routines and self-contained task teams.

1. *Directives* refer to the set of rules, standards, procedures and instructions for dealing with specific situations, such as hazardous waste disposal or handling of customer inquiries. Directives ensure standard and consistent responses to specific circumstances that frequently occur to an organisation.

2. *Organisational routines* refer to the development of task performance and coordination patterns, interaction protocols and process specifications in dealing with routine activities. Organisational

routines allow employees to apply and integrate their specialised knowledge to carry out their responsibilities and solve business problems.

3. *Self-contained task teams* are formed for problem-solving in uncertain and complex situations which prevent the specification of directives and organisational routines. Typically, these teams are made up of individuals with special knowledge and skills.

However, as the problems experienced by organisations that operate in the new economy are increasingly complex and dynamic in nature, standard solutions used to solve simple and ordinary problems are generally not applicable. New problem-solving skills, such as systems thinking and dynamics, may become a key qualification for new knowledge development. *Systems dynamics* is a computational technique for making cause-and-effect relationships operational. Its main tool is stock and flow diagrams, effectively a visual simulation programming language. There are multiple packages for developing simulations. Systems dynamics is used to further investigate problems that have been analysed with systems thinking, when quantitative analysis is required. It is used for systems analysis, scenario analysis and understanding rather than prediction.

Technology can have a positive influence on knowledge application (as discussed in Chapter 4) by facilitating the capture, updating and accessibility of organisational knowledge. It can increase the amount of organisational memory available, allow the application of knowledge across time and space, as well as enhance the speed of application through automation. Technology also supports knowledge application by embedding 'best practices' into organisational routines. While the best practice approach is efficient in handling routine situations, it is important that organisational members remain sensitive to contextual factors and consider the specific circumstances of the current environment when applying knowledge.

Conditions for knowledge application

Companies that have world-class processes for developing new knowledge may still fail. This is because the possession of knowledge does not automatically guarantee its successful application in daily work. There are a number of factors that hinder the effective use of knowledge in the everyday activities of an organisation. They may arise from organisational blindness, fear of revealing one's own weaknesses or a general mistrust of outside knowledge.

Therefore, appropriate measures must be taken to ensure that valuable skills and knowledge assets are effectively utilised. These are briefly discussed below:

1. *Meeting the needs of users.* When information systems are left unused or project reports unread, it is often because they do not meet the needs of the users. Many studies show that individuals usually make use of knowledge based on convenience and ease of use. A good way to encourage use is to make the knowledge infrastructure user-friendly. Some of the features that make systems user-friendly are simplicity, timeliness and compatibility. This means that the required knowledge should be localised and transferred simply and quickly and should be made available in the form that permits prompt application and continued use.

   In general, the organisational knowledge base can be used with greater effectiveness if it offers ready access to interesting information and knowledge, gives guidelines on how it can be obtained, and is current and of high quality. A software program that offers little noticeable improvement will often be ignored, as will a scientific memo on an irrelevant topic. The key issue is finding the right balance between the cost of obtaining and the benefit of using the knowledge.

2. *Fostering a supportive working environment.* User-friendly workspaces can encourage the use of knowledge. Proximity to the required knowledge can be achieved by the positioning of workstations and sections to allow easier communication or exchange between individuals or sections. Open and flexible layouts with fewer offices and more shared work and conference spaces that can be used by many people at different times are also useful. Making individual offices and workshops more attractive are other simple ways of creating an atmosphere that encourages use of knowledge. New knowledge will be applied more readily in a context of collective problem solving.

   Some organisations use designated physical spaces, usually located at the central points of the office building, to serve as centres to encourage knowledge exchange and utilisation. Such centres provide opportunities for the graphical presentation of material in the form of wall, video or interactive displays. The contents can include news and messages from different projects and people, and provide a type of 'ideas market'. This makes these places inviting and enables employees to identify and access the knowledge they need, thus encouraging and fostering its application.

Conclusion

This chapter describes the four generic knowledge processes: knowledge creation, knowledge storage/retrieval, knowledge sharing/transfer and knowledge utilisation. For the sake of convenience, we discuss these in sequence. However, it is important to note that these four processes are not a discrete, independent and monolithic set of activities. They are instead dynamic, interdependent and interconnected (Alavi and Leidner, 2001).

In practice, organisations do not create, store, transfer and apply knowledge in a linear order. For example, knowledge might be applied on the job immediately after it is created, hence bypassing the processes of storage and transfer. In addition, the creation of new knowledge might be triggered by the application of existing knowledge in a new context. Nonetheless, the four knowledge processes discussed in this chapter are essential to effective organisational knowledge management (Alavi and Leidner, 2001). The proposition is that the systematic and integrative management of these processes will lead to successful KM outcomes. These outcomes are discussed in Chapter 7.

Note

1. There are a number of classification schemes, such as the five-step knowledge evolution cycle by Wiig (1999), the four sub-processes scheme by Alavi and Leidner (2001) or the three sub-processes classification by Grover and Davenport (2001). Alavi and Leidner (2001) note that no major conceptual difference exists between different classification schemes. The difference lies mainly in terms of the number and labelling of processes rather than the underlying concepts.

References

Alavi, M. and Leidner, D.E. (2001) 'Knowledge management and knowledge management systems: conceptual foundations and research issues', *MIS Quarterly*, 25 (1): 107–36.

Davenport, T.H. and Glaser, J. (2002) 'Just-in-time delivery comes to knowledge management', *Harvard Business Review*, 80 (7): 107–11.

Grant, R.M. (1996) 'Toward a knowledge-based theory of the firm', *Strategic Management Journal*, 17 (Winter Special Issue): 109–22.

Grover, V. and Davenport, T.H. (2001) 'General perspectives on knowledge management: fostering a research agenda', *Journal of Management Information System*, 18 (1): 5–21.

Holtham, C. and Courtney, N. (1998) 'The executive learning ladder: a knowledge creation process grounded in the strategic information systems domain', in *Proceedings of the Fourth American Conference on Information Systems*, Baltimore, MD, August.

Inkpen, A. and Dikur, I. (1998) 'Knowledge management processes and international joint ventures', *Organisation Science*, 9 (4): 454–68.

Marakas, G. (1999) *Decision Support System for the 21st Century*. Englewood Cliffs, NJ: Prentice Hall.

Markus, A. (2001) 'Towards a theory of knowledge reuse: types of knowledge reuse situations and factors in reuse success', *Journal of Management Information Systems*, 18 (1): 57–93.

Nonaka, I. and Konno, N. (1998) 'The concept of "ba": building a foundation for knowledge creation', *California Management Review*, 40 (3): 40–54.

Nonaka, I. and Takeuchi, H. (1995) *The Knowledge Creating Company: How Japanese Companies Create the Dynamics of Innovation*. New York: Oxford University Press.

Pentland, B.T. (1995) 'Information systems and organisational learning: the social epistemology of organisational knowledge systems', *Accounting, Management and Information Technologies*, 5 (1): 1–21.

Probst, G.J.B., Raub, S. and Romhart, K. (2000) *Managing Knowledge*. Chichester: Wiley.

Stein, E.W. and Zwass, V. (1995) 'Actualising organisational memory with information systems', *Information Systems Research*, 6 (2): 85–117.

Walsh, J.P. and Ungson, G.R. (1991) 'Organisational memory', *Academy of Management Review*, 16 (1): 57–91.

Wiig, K.M. (1999) *Knowledge Management: An Emerging Discipline Rooted in a Long History*. Available at: *http://www.krii.com/downloads/km_emerg_discipl.pdf* (accessed 2 April 2004).

Wilkins, A.L. and Bristow, N.J. (1987) 'For successful organisational culture, honor your past', *Academy of Management Executive*, 1: 221–9.

6

Understanding knowledge as an asset

Introduction

In previous chapters, we have discussed the processes of knowledge creation, storage/search, transfer and application. We have also discussed various socio-organisational and technological interventions that enable and/or facilitate these knowledge processes. But, the question of what knowledge is strategically important to organisations and how knowledge can be managed strategically still remains unanswered.

Throughout this book, we have argued that the ultimate aim of KM is to create or add value to an organisation, its customers and stakeholders, by harnessing the knowledge resident in an organisation. To make strategic business decisions and take effective actions, and to attain the goals of innovation and competitiveness, organisations need to know not only what they know, but also what they need to know. Furthermore, different types of knowledge may dominate in different organisations, and different organisations may require different types of knowledge. Hence, an important challenge for a company is to determine what type of knowledge is best suited for its particular needs.

In this chapter, we address these issues. First, we review, contrast and synthesise various views regarding knowledge in the literature. We then present a widely agreed view of knowledge as a strategic asset before we conclude with the issue of the strategic management of knowledge.

Perspectives on knowledge

Defining knowledge is no easy task. Knowledge is a complex and ambiguous concept that has generated wide debate in the literature. Therefore, the understanding and management of knowledge should not be approached from a single point of view. Rather, one should consider knowledge from multiple perspectives. The following perspectives are predominantly based on those presented by Holsapple (2003).

Data vs information vs knowledge

The most common knowledge perspective adopted by the IS community takes a hierarchical view of data, information and knowledge. From this perspective, knowledge is at the top of the data–information–knowledge hierarchy. Data are isolated facts, information is meaningful and processed data, and knowledge is information that is actionable. This perspective is contrasted by Devlin (1999), who promotes a view of data as encoded knowledge, and information as an encoding/decoding scheme necessary to extract knowledge from the code.

Knowledge states

The knowledge states perspective further extends the data–information–knowledge hierarchy. It suggests a continuum of knowledge stages that reflect the variations in an individual's progression from the lowest to the highest level of knowledge. For example, the six-stage model of knowledge shown below identifies a set of six knowledge states and operations that need to be undertaken to progress from one state to another. Thus, by gathering data, and then analysing and synthesising information, one can get a deeper insight, and subsequently make better judgements and decisions about an issue of interest.

Knowledge progression operations and states

gather → DATA → select → INFORMATION → analyse → STRUCTURED INFORMATION → synthesise → INSIGHT → weigh → JUDGEMENT → evaluate → DECISION

Source: Holsapple (2003).

Thing vs human

The systems perspective of knowledge sees knowledge as an object that can be codified and then stored in a computerised system. The implication is that knowledge can be separated from its source and context. From this perspective, the fundamental purpose of a KM initiative is to acquire, capture, access and reuse codified knowledge throughout the organisation. An alternative view suggests that knowledge can only reside in people's minds. From this perspective, KM allows individual knowledge seekers to identify and communicate with knowledge sources (human experts) to acquire and exchange knowledge. The goal of KM is to create a connected environment for knowledge exchange and transfer.

Individual vs group

The implication of the knowledge exchange perspective of KM is that collective knowledge is seen simply as the sum of knowledge of individual members in a group or an organisation. However, the group perspective of knowledge recognises that collective knowledge is often more than just the sum of individual knowledge, due to team learning and development that is different to the collection of individual capabilities. Thus the goal of knowledge management is to promote collaboration and synergistic relationships among team members, rather than just knowledge exchange.

Stock vs flow

Knowledge can also be viewed in terms of stocks or flows. Knowledge stocks are seen as inventories of knowledge available to one or more processors. An organisation that embraces a stock (or structural) perspective will typically develop knowledge stores (or repositories) and will try to capture the organisation's knowledge by using software.

Flow (or processual) perspective is focused on the movement of knowledge from one stock to another or on the use of knowledge in a stock to produce new knowledge. The flow perspective also emphasises that knowledge is socially constructed and embedded in practice.

An organisation that adopts this perspective considers that knowledge resides in the minds of people and that a substantial part of an individual's tacit knowledge always remains tacit. Thus, managing knowledge becomes managing people and the interactions among them.

Representation vs construction

The positivist perspective views knowledge as 'justified true belief'. This privileged status of knowledge as fundamental truth and the representation of reality has been questioned lately. Postmodernists have emphasised the social and cultural situatedness of knowledge and the negotiation process used to test and refine what is accepted as knowledge.

Tacit vs explicit

Nonaka and Takeuchi (1995) defined tacit knowledge as personal knowledge that is embedded in individual experience. It involves intangible factors such as personal beliefs, perspectives and value systems. It is highly idiosyncratic, contextual and hard to articulate. Such a view of tacit knowledge belongs to the so-called difficulty school of thought, which can be best summarised by Polanyi's well-known claim 'we know more than we can tell' (Polanyi, 1958). On the other hand, the de facto school of thought maintains that all knowledge in people's heads is tacit as long as it has not yet been articulated (Hedesstrom and Whitley, 2000).

Explicit knowledge is defined as knowledge that is easily articulated in formal language including grammatical statements, mathematical expressions, specifications, manuals and so forth (Nonaka and Takeuchi, 1995). It is externalised knowledge usually codified in databases, and thus easily communicated and shared. Some researchers suggest that explicit knowledge is equated with information (Stenmark, 2002; Sveiby, 1997).

Propositional vs prescriptive

A distinction can also be drawn between propositional (declarative, cognitive and know-that) and prescriptive (procedural, technical and know-how) knowledge (Mokyr, 2003). The former is knowledge that catalogues phenomena of interest and their regularities. It relates to statements of facts (what things are). The latter is the knowledge that prescribes actions for the manipulation of these phenomena. It relates to techniques and sets of instructions or recipes (how to do things) that may be expressed in algorithmic ways.

Known vs unknown

One of the most recent additions to knowledge taxonomies is Snowden's classification of known, knowable, complex and chaos (Snowden, 2002). The key proposition is that the known domain is best managed by including evidence-based, proven best practices. Business processes can be used as a good source of the knowable. It is the domain of good practice where knowledge models can be developed given the resources, capability and time. The complex domain can be best understood and managed in terms of patterns. The patterns are defined as emergent properties of the interaction of the various agents. Chaos represents the realm of the completely unknown and uncharted. For managing chaos one requires creative and innovative ideas that would impose new order. In short, the nature of knowledge is key to understanding the knowledge process (or narrative), and the effectiveness of this process depends on the knowledge context.

Good vs bad

To be of value, knowledge should be used for a purpose. The economic perspective views knowledge as a useful saleable product or commodity, a possession to be protected, sold and capitalised upon. By knowing more rather than less organisations are more likely to succeed. The implication of this is that knowledge management is instrumental in creating wealth by enabling organisations to better manage their knowledge assets. On the other hand, there are fears that the proliferation of new knowledge can be abused and used in ways that can have negative effects on economic welfare. Responding to such fears, Mokyr (2003) argues that although knowledge is full of dangers and pitfalls, so is ignorance. He also suggests that useful knowledge based on wide epistemic bases has the ability to adjust, improve and self-correct.

Case study 6.1

On what knowledge do organisations rely: explicit or tacit?

Hansen et al. (1999) have found that effective firms excel by focusing primarily on one type of knowledge (explicit or tacit) and using the other in a supporting role, rather than trying to use both to an equal degree.

In general, they have found that large consulting firms such as Andersen consulting and Ernst & Young compete by providing expertise in high-quality, reliable and fast information system implementations by reusing codified knowledge. They tend to rely on explicit knowledge. Typically, these firms develop knowledge objects by removing client-sensitive information, and by pulling key pieces of knowledge (e.g. interview guides, work schedules, benchmark data and market analyses) out of the documents and then storing them in electronic repositories for future search and reuse without the need to contact the originating human experts. The argument is that codification opens up the possibility of achieving scale in knowledge reuse and of growing business through reuse. To ensure that the codification process is efficient, these firms invest heavily in IT in order to connect people with reusable codified knowledge.

In contrast, strategy consulting firms such as Bain, the Boston Consulting Group and McKinsey focus primarily on tacit knowledge. These companies compete by providing creative, analytically rigorous advice on high level strategic problems by channelling individual expertise. In their KM approach, knowledge is transferred in brainstorming sessions and in one-to-one conversations. Consultants collectively arrive at deeper insights by an iterative process of generating and evaluating ideas on problems they need to solve. To make this approach work well, these companies typically invest in building networks of people so that tacit knowledge can be shared. They invest moderately in IT mainly to facilitate conversations and foster people networks in many different ways (e.g. by supporting a culture in which consultants talk with colleagues face to face or over the telephone, via e-mail and via video-conferences; by transferring people between offices; by creating directories of expertise; and by using consulting directors to assist project teams).

Source: Hansen et al. (1999).

Knowledge classification systems

The above review reveals that knowledge is perceived differently by different people. Understanding different perspectives of knowledge helps us gain a better understanding of the multifaceted nature of knowledge. In this way, a knowledge worker can better justify his or her own knowledge portfolio selection. Such a consideration can also highlight knowledge facets that a knowledge manager might consider in designing and overseeing a KM initiative.

In order to make sense of the variety of perspectives of knowledge that exist in the literature, we use Johnston's (1998) knowledge classification systems shown in Table 6.1 as a context for further discussion. Knowledge classification systems are grouped into three main clusters: administrative-pragmatic, epistemologically sourced and economically orientated classifications.

Administrative-pragmatic classifications

Administrative-pragmatic classifications represent a picture of knowledge stocks and flows. Examples include knowledge about customers, products, processes and competitors. Such knowledge might also include

| **Table 6.1** | Knowledge classification systems |

	Administrative-pragmatic	Epistemologically sourced	Economically orientated
Focus/ description	Represent useful knowledge stocks and flows	Sophisticated and scientifically grounded	Recognise competitive or survival value of knowledge
Examples/ knowledge types	Basic, applied Product, customer, competitor, etc. Data, information, knowledge, wisdom hierarchy	Object, personal Embrained, embodied, encultured, embedded, encoded Formal, instrumental, informal, contingent, tacit, meta-knowledge	Employee competence, internal structure, external structure Know-what, why, who, when, where, how
Applications/ benefits	Auditing, accounting, reporting	Research, improved understanding	Economic activity, strategic planning

technology and business frameworks, project experiences and the tools used to implement a process.

Epistemologically sourced classifications

Epistemologically sourced classifications have largely emerged from the sociology of scientific knowledge. They offer more sophisticated and grounded categories of knowledge. Within this classification, there are two ways of grouping knowledge: Blackler's (1995) five knowledge categories and Fleck's (1997) six categories. Blackler's classification includes: embrained (abstract, scientific), embodied (action-orientated, transmitted face to face and rooted in context), encultured (shared understanding, socially constructed), embedded (residing in routines, relationships and technology) and encoded (recorded in signs and symbols, distilled) knowledge categories.

Fleck's classification distinguishes among: formal (coded, acquired through formal learning), instrumental (embodied in tool use, learnt through practice), informal (embodied in verbal interaction, learnt through interaction in context), contingent (context specific, acquired by on-the-spot learning), tacit (embodied in people, learned through experience and mentorship) and meta-knowledge (embodied in organisational values, acquired through socialisation) categories. Handzic and Hasan (2003) suggest that epistemologically sourced classifications hold considerable promise for the improved understanding of knowledge management and the development of better models for KM.

Economically orientated classifications

Economically orientated approaches to the classification of knowledge focus on economically useful definitions. In general, these classifications help improve our understanding of knowledge contribution and provide instrumental guidance to economic activity. Examples include Sveiby's (1997) intangible assets of a company in terms of its employee competence, internal structure and external structure. The alternative classification proposed by Lundvall and Johnson (1994) includes know-what, why, who, when, where and how categories. This system acknowledges that each of the categories contributes to achieving desired outcomes in the appropriate context.

Organisational knowledge assets

Consistent with the economically orientated view of knowledge, the term 'knowledge asset' is used in this chapter to denote a knowledge-based resource of a firm which enables its products and services to be provided, thus ensuring that it has a viable economic life within industry and market context. Knowledge asset is synonymous with intellectual capital, intellectual assets or intangible assets (Guthrie, 2001). As defined in Chapter 2, knowledge assets or IC refer to intellectual material in its various forms that drives growth and value creation for an organisation.

There are many classification schemes which attempt to categorise knowledge assets or IC in organisations. In Chapter 3, we presented a widely accepted scheme of three sub-categories: human capital, organisational (internal) capital and customer (external) capital. In addition to this, knowledge assets can be divided into core and supporting assets.

Core knowledge assets comprise a firm's core skills and competencies. They lie in the areas in which the firm has competitive strengths. They represent the cognitive characteristics of an organisation and its collective functional knowledge (Hatten and Rosenthal, 2001). Examples of core knowledge assets include know-how, insight, judgement, experience of employees, expertise, organisational culture, social relationships and networks, intellectual property rights, patents, copyrights, contracts, licences, trademarks, registered designs, trade secrets and reputation. To gain a sustainable advantage in a competitive environment, these competencies are typically dominant and hard to imitate or substitute.

In contrast, supporting knowledge assets are complementary generic and operational assets that support or enable the delivery, storage and acquisition of core knowledge assets. Examples include organisational structure and infrastructure such as information systems and databases. Generally, supporting knowledge assets are relatively easy to imitate (Jones, 2001; Pemberton and Stonehouse, 2000).

Knowledge assets portfolio

Every organisation possesses valuable intellectual materials in the form of data, documents, procedures, capabilities, etc. These can be found in people, organisational structures and processes and customer relationships. To succeed, organisations need to have a clear understanding of which knowledge assets are important to their success and how these assets are distributed over different parts of the company and among different functions and workers. According to Grant (1991), the portfolio of knowledge assets is typically determined by an organisation's strategic plan.

The following sections present some examples of knowledge assets under each IC category.

People (human capital)

A significant proportion of a company's knowledge assets is often stored in the minds of its employees. The work of highly skilled employees has been widely recognised as an important factor in value creation. When organisational knowledge is concentrated in the minds of individuals, some workers can become irreplaceable, and if they leave the company, their departure may create gaps that are extremely difficult to fill. Mishaps of this kind emphasise the need for vital competencies to be carefully identified and evaluated.

While the individual abilities of knowledge workers form the basis of successful company activity, the success of many projects and strategies also depends on whether different knowledge workers and different components in the knowledge base can be combined efficiently. Collective knowledge, which is more than the sum of individual knowledge, is particularly important to the long-term survival and success of a company.

Knowledge artefacts (organisational capital)

Some organisational knowledge is manifested in the form of artefacts. Examples of knowledge artefacts are videotapes, books, memos, business plans, manuals, patents and products. Representing knowledge in an artefact involves the embodiment of that knowledge in an object, thus positively affecting its ability to be transferred, shared and preserved.

Structural and procedural assets (organisational capital)

This kind of organisational knowledge is manifested in the organisation's actual behaviours: its culture, infrastructure, purpose and strategy. The cultural knowledge resource comprises basic assumptions and beliefs that govern participants' activities. An organisation's culture can be recognised by observing participants' behaviours, such as knowledge sharing, tolerance for failure, attitudes towards risk-taking and encouragement of experimentation.

Knowledge embodied in an organisation's infrastructure structures participants' roles, the relationships between co-workers and the regulations that govern the use of roles and relationships. Roles knowledge defines what needs to be done by different participants. Relationships knowledge is about understanding the types of available interactions that are permissible and effective. Regulations constitute knowledge about formal rules and procedures that participants are expected to observe. Finally, purpose and strategy knowledge defines an organisation's reason for existence (e.g. its mission, vision, objectives and goals) and a plan to achieve its purpose in an effective manner (e.g. how to use the organisation's resources to promote a product).

Customer relationship (customer capital)

Knowledge about customers and the external environment including the market that the organisation serves is a valuable asset. Such an asset can become a critical factor in determining a firm's competitive edge in a mature and highly competitive market environment.

Knowledge strategy

All organisations formulate and implement competitive strategic plans to close the gap between what a firm can do and what a firm must do to be competitive (Zack, 1999). Similarly, organisations need to formulate and implement knowledge strategies to close the gap between what a firm knows and what a firm must know to be competitive, and to align the knowledge strategy with the firm's business strategy.

In general, a knowledge strategy defines the actions necessary to ensure that the organisation's knowledge assets meet and support organisational business objectives. Typically, it includes actions to determine which knowledge assets are possessed and required, which changes or adaptations to existing knowledge assets are needed, actions to dispose of obsolete knowledge assets that are no longer economically viable, and actions to acquire and develop new knowledge assets.

There are a number of methods and tools available to help organisations formulate knowledge strategies. Case study 6.2 describes how Siemens AG developed its knowledge strategy.

Case study 6.2

Knowledge strategy process (KSP) at Siemens AG

Siemens AG introduced the knowledge strategy process (KSP) into the corporation as a method for business owners and their teams to determine and integrate knowledge strategy and action plans into the business strategy process. KSP identifies which knowledge areas have an impact on the business, how strong this impact is and which deficits there are in each area, and determines what management should do in response to these issues. Actions that solve issues in several knowledge areas or across business are the major output of a specific knowledge strategy (KS). These actions in turn are a valuable requirement input to the KM strategy or roadmap concerned with the development and implementation of socio-technological solutions required by a knowledge strategy.

The Siemens AG's KSP consists of six basic steps which result in a KM action and project plan. These steps lead from the currently most relevant business perspective for the near future, to KM actions being focused by business objectives and orchestrated across all knowledge-related management disciplines. More specifically, the KS process starts with determining the most relevant business context, strategies and ambitions for the near future. This may be a new product line, a process innovation or a business or organisational transformation.

In the next step, the related key performance indicators (KPIs) are identified. Examples include customer success, a performance index for project execution, employee satisfaction and an innovation index. The process continues with identifying key knowledge areas relevant for the business case and their impact on the current and future KPIs. These typically constitute

10–12 thematic consolidations of experiences, theories, findings and abilities in their various manifestations. In the following step, the identified knowledge area states (as-is and to-be) are assessed in terms of proficiency, diffusion and codification in order to ascertain the fitness between the actual and targeted status. Finally, KM actions are defined to achieve to-be states for prioritised knowledge areas.

Source: Hofer-Alfeis and van der Spek (2002).

A more complex process that includes both the competitive strategy and the knowledge strategy has been proposed by Zack (2001). Zack terms it the knowledge-based strategy. The first component, competitive strategy, describes the actions required to manage the firm's business, create products and satisfy customers. The second component, KM strategy, describes the actions required to manage the knowledge environment, knowledge gaps and redundant or obsolete knowledge assets. The knowledge-based strategy is preceded by the strategic KM involving the collection and analysis of strategic information on the firm, industry and market.

Handzic (2004) also incorporates elements of a knowledge strategy into the comprehensive practical KM method. This method starts with awareness building and determining the business motives for KM initiatives. It continues by recommending organisations to take stock of their existing knowledge and where it resides, and to evaluate it to determine remaining gaps and changing needs using a well defined measurement system. It finishes with the suggestion to implement those KM solutions that combine processes, environment and technology that have the best potential to enhance knowledge and add value to the firm.

Organisations should make sure that there are two important alignments in the process of developing a knowledge strategy – first, the alignment of IC elements or knowledge assets with strategic objectives and second, the alignment of KM processes with each IC element (Zhou and Fink, 2003; Zhou, 2004). The first alignment is important as it helps to identify the main drivers of value creation. The second alignment is equally important as this will ensure that KM initiatives contribute to the development of IC or knowledge assets. Through this approach, IC elements serve as critical success factors (CSF) that bridge the pursuit of strategic objectives and effective KM processes. Once critical success factors are identified, a number of key performance indicators can then be defined for each KM process.

The above approach is developed based on the linkage between IC assets and KM processes. Historically, intellectual capital and knowledge management have been pursued separately, with overlapping activities. This is reflected in the fragmentation of the existing KM literature. In their award winning paper, Zhou and Fink (2003) developed a systematic approach to linking them through the intellectual capital web (ICW). The linkage between IC and KM is based on the existence of differences, similarities and complementariness between intellectual capital management and knowledge management. For more discussions on the relationship between IC and KM, interested readers are referred to Zhou and Fink (2003).

Conclusion

This chapter has explored ways of looking at knowledge, knowledge assets and knowledge strategy. Knowledge is a complex and multifaceted concept. It is also an essential asset of modern organisations for delivering the products and services that justify their existence and enable their success or survival in the new economy.

The pursuit of different business objectives requires the development of different types of knowledge resources, strengths, process capabilities and organisational structures. In order for these knowledge assets to be effective, the organisation's knowledge portfolio must be aligned with its business strategy. The role of knowledge strategy is to determine those knowledge assets that have a high impact on the business, to identify potential deficits and to determine what management should do to resolve these issues.

References

Blackler, F. (1995) 'Knowledge, knowledge work and organizations: an overview and interpretation', *Organization Studies*, 16: 1021–46.

Devlin, K. (1999) *Infosense: Turning Information into Knowledge*. New York: W.H. Freeman.

Fleck, J. (1997) 'Contingent knowledge and technology development', *Technology Analysis and Strategic Management*, 9 (4).

Grant, R.M. (1991) 'The resource-based theory of competitive advantage: implications for strategy formation', *California Management Review*, 33 (3): 114–35.

Guthrie, J. (2001) 'The management, the measurement and the reporting of intellectual capital', *Journal of Intellectual Capital*, 2 (1): 27–41.

Handzic, M. (2004) 'Knowledge management in SMEs: practical guidelines', *Asia Pacific Tech Monitor*, January–February: 29–34.

Handzic, M. and Hasan, H. (2003) 'The search for an integrated KM framework', in H. Hasan and M. Handzic (eds), *Australian Studies in Knowledge Management*. Wollongong: UOW Press, pp. 3–34.

Hansen, M.T., Nohria, N. and Tierney, T. (1999) 'What's your strategy for managing knowledge?', *Harvard Business Review*, 77 (2): 106–16.

Hatten, K.J. and Rosenthal, S.R. (2001) *Reaching for the Knowledge Edge*. New York: AMACOM.

Hedesstrom, T. and Whitley, E.A. (2000) 'What is meant by tacit knowledge? Towards a better understanding of the shape of actions', in *Proceedings of the European Conference on Knowledge Management (ECKM 2000)*.

Hofer-Alfeis, J. and van der Spek, R. (2002) 'The knowledge strategy process – an instrument for business owners', in T.H. Davenport and G.J.B. Probst (eds), *Knowledge Management Case Book*. Erlangen: Publics and John Wiley & Sons, pp. 24–39.

Holsapple, C.W. (2003) 'Knowledge and its attributes', in C.W. Holsapple (ed.), *Handbook on Knowledge Management*. Berlin: Springer, pp. 165–88.

Johnston, R. (1998) *The Changing Nature and Forms of Knowledge: A Review*. Canberra: Department of Employment, Education, Training and Youth Affairs.

Jones, B.K. (2001) *Knowledge Management: A Quantitative Study into People's Perceptions and Expectations in the Developing Knowledge Economy*. Southern Cross University.

Lundvall, B. and Johnson, B. (1994) 'The learning economy', *Journal of Industry Studies*, 1: 23–42.

Mokyr, J. (2003) *The Knowledge Society*, Ad Hoc Expert Group Meeting on Knowledge Systems and Development, United Nations, New York, 4–5 September.

Nonaka, I. and Takeuchi, H. (1995) *The Knowledge Creating Company: How Japanese Companies Create the Dynamics of Innovation*. New York: Oxford University Press.

Pemberton, J. D. and Stonehouse, G.H. (2000) 'Organisational learning and knowledge assets – an essential partnership', *Learning Organization: An International Journal*, 7 (4): 184–94.

Polanyi, M. (1958) *Personal Knowledge*. Chicago: University of Chicago Press.

Snowden, D. (2002) 'Complex acts of knowing: paradox and descriptive self-awareness', in *Proceedings of the European Conference on Knowledge Management (ECKM 2002)*, Dublin, September.

Stenmark, D. (2002) 'Information vs knowledge: the role of intranets in knowledge management', in *35th Hawaii International Conference on System Sciences*, Hawaii.

Sveiby, K.-E (1997) *The New Organizational Wealth: Managing and Measuring Knowledge Based Assets*. San Francisco: Berrett-Koehler.

Zack, M. (1999) 'Developing a knowledge strategy', *California Management Review*, 41 (3): 125–45.

Zack, M. (2001) *Developing a Knowledge Strategy: Epilogue*. Available at: *http://web.cba.neu.edu/~mzack/articles/kstrat2/kstrat2.htm* (accessed 13 December 2004).

Zhou, A. (2004) 'Managing knowledge strategically: a comparison of managers' perceptions between the private and public sector in Australia', *Journal of Information and Knowledge Management*, 3 (3): 1–10.

Zhou, A. and Fink, D. (2003) 'The intellectual capital web: a systematic linking of intellectual capital and knowledge management', *Journal of Intellectual Capital*, 4 (1): 34–48.

Part 3
Benefits and limitations of KM

7

Outcomes of KM

Introduction

Due to the complex nature of KM, managing knowledge well in an organisation can be difficult. It can also be quite expensive. Early KM adopters spent between 2.5 per cent and 10 per cent of their revenue on KM (Davenport et al., 1998). However, the potential gains for the organisations are rewarding. The most significant include improvement in organisational decision-making and innovation (Snowden, 2003), as well as productivity, agility and reputation (Holsapple and Singh, 2003). In general, effective knowledge management plays a key role in harnessing organisational knowledge resources, and thus determining an organisation's competitive advantage.

The dynamic capabilities approach provides a promising theoretical framework for exploring and appreciating the impacts of knowledge on competitiveness (Teece and Pisano, 2003). This framework emphasises two important aspects. First, the term 'dynamic' refers to the shifting character of the environment and the need for organisational adaptation. Second, the term 'capabilities' emphasises the key role of management in appropriately adapting, integrating and reconfiguring internal and external organisational skills, resources and functional competencies in a changing environment. From the dynamic capabilities approach, competitive success arises from the continuous development, exploitation and protection of a firm's assets. It also emphasises the importance of these capabilities being rooted in high-performance routines operating inside the firm, embedded in the firm's processes and conditioned by its history.

Currently, many organisations are initiating KM programmes or projects. It is important to note that KM should not be considered a one-off activity, but an ongoing process towards becoming a smarter organisation. It is also important to note that, given the nature of issues that KM attempts to address, it might be hard to anticipate the immediate benefits from a KM initiative. To achieve the desired outcomes, organisations need to have a clear picture of what they wish to achieve, as well as be realistic about their expectations. The literature suggests that the winners in the global marketplace demonstrate timely responsiveness, rapid and flexible product innovation and management capabilities to effectively coordinate and redeploy internal and external competencies (Teece and Pisano, 2003).

In Chapter 2 we alluded to the fact that KM can impact organisational performance in a number of ways. These can be grouped into three broad categories: risk minimisation, efficiency improvement and innovation (Von Krogh et al., 2000). We also mentioned that competitive strategies for these differ. This chapter will consider three aspects of the outcomes of KM: *knowledge retention* as a way of risk minimisation, *productivity improvement* as a way to improve performance efficiency and effectiveness, and *innovation* of products and processes. The chapter will also attempt to identify successful KM strategies and current practices leading to these outcomes.

Major KM outcomes

Knowledge retention

Knowledge loss is one of the major issues for knowledge-based organisations due to high employee turnover or retirement. According to Frank (2002), the chances are that the best employees will leave a company within four years. As for the public sector, knowledge loss is also a serious problem in the face of retirement of senior civil servants. Once these employees walk out of the door, valuable knowledge in their heads will go with them. Therefore, organisations in both the private and public sector are increasingly concerned about how to best retain knowledge.

It is argued that knowledge management can offer a solution to knowledge loss in an organisation through appropriate knowledge management processes and knowledge retention strategies. According to Von Krogh et al. (2000), if the prime motive for knowledge management is minimising risk from knowledge loss, the response typically involves identifying and holding on to the core competencies that the company has. Thus risk minimisation is closely related to knowledge initiatives aimed at locating and capturing valuable organisational knowledge. Because people are recognised as key holders of valuable knowledge in organisations, identifying, locating and capturing what is known by individuals and groups of employees is of critical importance for business survival.

Essentially, knowledge retention in the organisation is a knowledge exploitation process (Hansen et al., 1999). It is concerned with knowledge sharing to retain the existing knowledge by using different tools and techniques. The main concern is how to tap the brains of employees who are retiring, moving to new jobs or leaving the organisation, and convert their tacit knowledge into explicit knowledge to be further recorded and stored in the organisational memory for easy use or reuse throughout the organisation (Handzic and Bewsell, 2003). For example, documented project management knowledge, expertise and skills accumulated in the construction industry were found to benefit both employees and the public at large (Land et al., 2002). At a higher level, society's knowledge records are preserving the cultural capital of nations (Handzic, 2003).

KM can also impact people's learning, adaptability and job satisfaction (Becerra-Fernandez et al., 2004). For example, KM can facilitate employees' creativity and group effectiveness through informal and formal socialisation (Handzic and Chaimungkalanont, 2003). In short, knowledge sharing and leveraging what is already in place in the organisation is one of the most important aspects of knowledge management.

To avoid organisational brain-drain, managers need to develop and implement effective knowledge retention strategies aligned with their overall KM strategies. Frank (2002) suggests five strategies to improve knowledge retention in organisations. These are retaining the best people; mentoring and coaching; sharing best practices; sharing lessons learnt and documentation.

The easiest way to reduce knowledge loss is to avoid losing it in the first place. Given that the most valuable knowledge in an organisation often resides in the minds of its employees, the obvious way to retain this knowledge is to retain the people who have the knowledge. Strategies to improve employee retention include: offering increased pay, alternative career paths through job rotation and a flexible work environment such as telecommuting or part-time work.

Mentoring and coaching is a popular strategy for tacit knowledge transfer as discussed earlier. It allows new or less experienced employees to learn from more experienced senior personnel through working together and bonding. This strategy is particularly effective in situations of large employee populations approaching retirement, high employee turnover or steep learning curve requirements.

Sharing best practices assumes sharing of what worked for others and using that proven and tested knowledge to improve decision-making and conduct business faster and more reliably. One of the potential dangers for organisations adopting this strategy is the 'universalistic' understanding of the term best practice. This approach might give a false impression that there is only one best solution to the problem. The contingency perspective, in contrast, warns that the success of a KM strategy is highly context dependent. Organisations undertaking a best practice study should keep this in mind.

Sharing lessons learned allows organisations to tap into and share the experiential knowledge of its members. Typically, lessons learned are brief statements by teams or individuals about knowledge gained. They usually include both successes and failures. They can be shared through discussions at meetings and forums, or be available for online access in the lessons learned database.

Documentation has been discussed in the last chapter. Documenting the situation and reasons behind one's thinking can help retain the knowledge and experience of the decision-makers. However, the process may be costly and difficult, and is therefore often neglected. It also requires continuous maintenance to keep the content up to date. Nonetheless, the cost of rediscovering knowledge can be far greater than that of documenting it. The use of content management software packages is recommended to facilitate documentation.

Finally, before choosing any particular knowledge retention strategy, an organisation should develop an understanding of its own context, and select the method appropriate to its particular problem. It should also monitor the implementation of the strategy over time to ensure its effectiveness. Case study 7.1 illustrates one KM strategy and its outcomes at Ford Motors.

Case study 7.1

Ford Motors

Ford Motors has implemented a number of knowledge-sharing initiatives aimed at driving down the time it takes to get new models of cars and trucks from concept to full production. A best-practice replication programme shares process improvements among 37 plants around the globe. Individuals and groups suggest improvements by entering a brief description of their best practice into a database and each week the 37 plants receive several best practices that apply to that plant. Knowledge transfer is supplemented with face-to-face exchanges. Each best practice passes through a quality assurance process to ensure that the information can be trusted.

A range of approaches, including the use of intranets and collaboration tools such as videoconferencing, support the best-practice replication programme. In the five years after the programme was implemented more than 2,800 proven practices were shared, helping reduce concept-to-production time from 36 months to 24 months. The value of these improvements has been estimated at US$1.25 billion.

Source: Rollo and Clarke (2001).

Productivity improvement

In today's complex economy, businesses are constantly confronted with the need to operate more efficiently and effectively in order to stay competitive and satisfy increasing market demands. Wiig and Jooste (2003) consider competitive productivity or 'doing more with less' as a basic factor for the continued survival of any organisation or nation. They also distinguish between two important types of productivity: performance and economic productivity. Performance productivity involves improvements in workplace operations and products and services through the application of KM principles. Economic productivity involves financial gains that normally result from performance gains. However, managers need to recognise that improvements in economic productivity often depend more upon competitive and market contexts than merely increasing workers' performance productivity.

Generally, efficiency can be achieved by reducing consumption of resources (e.g. time, supplies) to produce more with the same inputs, and effectiveness can be improved by delivering better quality, reducing rework or identifying better ways of working. To this end, Wiig and Jooste (2003) suggest a number of ways in which improved knowledge can increase performance productivity.

Improving efficiency usually relates to knowledge initiatives for transferring experiences and best practices throughout the organisation in order to avoid unnecessary invention and to reduce cost. By applying appropriate knowledge, people are able to handle tasks more efficiently. This is closely linked to knowledge retention discussed above. KM can also help organisations become more effective by helping them select and perform the most appropriate processes and make the best possible decisions. KM can help organisations to avoid repeating past mistakes, foresee potential problems and reduce the need to modify plans (Becerra-Fernandez et al., 2004). Case study 7.2 illustrates how the South Australian Government applies KM to improve the effectiveness and efficiency of service delivery.

Case study 7.2

South Australian Government

Government agencies around the world are facing increasing community expectations of better social services and access to information resources. The challenge for government departments is to manage their internal environment to meet these changing and growing expectations. With 30,000 staff at 800 service locations, the South Australian Department of Human Services turned to knowledge management to deliver service improvement.

The Department adopted a holistic knowledge management strategy that focuses on people, business processes and enabling technologies. The goal was to integrate historically separate streams of health, housing and community services. A virtual corporate environment was developed using intranet and Internet services that facilitated collaboration and integration across disparate sources to deliver services.

A key element of the department's KM strategy was to leverage relationships with external stakeholders and customers. Strategies include the integrated analysis of socio-demographic and service usage statistics (previously fragmented). These analyses were used to build web-based knowledge resources. The outcome is that South Australian community and service providers were provided with equitable and widespread access to expert knowledge and were able to directly contact the right people for service delivery.

Source: Rollo and Clarke (2001).

Innovation

In addition to knowledge retention as a way of minimising risk, and improving business efficiency and effectiveness, knowledge management can enable innovation. KM can impact process innovations, value-added products and knowledge-based products (Becerra-Fernandez et al., 2004). New products and services resulting from the application of knowledge may bring profound changes in the way businesses operate and compete in the new economy.

The unifying thread among various theoretical views is the perception that innovation is the key driver of an organisation's long-term economic success. Innovation of products, processes and structures has been assessed as a critical component in business success in the twenty-first century. Successful innovative organisations often take a strategic view of knowledge, formulate knowledge visions, tear down knowledge barriers, develop new corporate values and trust, catalyse and coordinate knowledge creation, manage the various contexts, develop a conversational culture, globalise local knowledge and localise global knowledge (Nonaka and Nishiguchi, 2001). However, as Von Krogh et al. (2000) point out, the greatest challenge for organisations is to move toward knowledge-enabling by consciously and deliberately addressing knowledge management.

A study of best practices in knowledge management by Arthur Andersen (1998) reveals the following common characteristics of innovative organisations:

- risk-taking and experimentation are encouraged;
- uncertainty and ambiguity are tolerated;
- failure is not punished but is viewed as an opportunity for learning;
- the organisation fosters an 'entrepreneurial spirit' and employees are given the time, resources and support to pursue new ideas;
- the process of relearning and unlearning is considered critical to generating products and services that meet current and future market needs;
- both internal and external competition serve as a catalyst for new ideas;
- successful innovations are celebrated enthusiastically;
- creativity-boosting techniques, brainstorming sessions, 'agendaless' meetings and scenario planning help surface unexpected solutions.

Case study 7.3 provides a good example of such an organisation.

Case study 7.3

Pfiser

Competition to reach markets first in the pharmaceutical industry is intense and Pfizer is using knowledge management practices to beat the industry average.

Of US$1.7 billion annually spent in research (1996 figures), only one in seven million screened compounds ever made it to market. Pfizer recognised that if it could manage the research process more efficiently it would have a significant competitive advantage.

Pfizer's main approach involved the data mining of scientific publications and other databases to make researchers aware of progress and projects by other researchers. An example of its success was the discovery of the famous impotence treatment Viagra. Viagra was originally designed as a drug to fight angina but nurses recorded an unusual side effect during trials. The side effect was identified by a clinician when analysing the results.

Source: Rollo and Clarke (2001).

Other outcomes

Other possible outcomes of KM include customer intimacy, product-to-market excellence, operational excellence (O'Dell et al., 2003), reputation (Holsapple and Singh, 2003), employee learning and satisfaction, impacts on processes and products, direct and indirect impacts on organisational performance through advertising and demonstrating intellectual leadership in industry (Becerra-Fernandez et al., 2004) and increases in revenue and profit (Earl, 2001).

Some researchers argue that KM can also help organisations become more agile. According to Dove (2003), agility derives from the firm's ability to act and the intellectual ability to understand appropriate things to act upon. Today, organisations are finding it increasingly difficult to adapt to the instability and uncertainty in their business environment. The knowledge base is exploding and knowledge becomes obsolete faster. Hence, if useful knowledge is not deployed quickly enough, it can become obsolete before it generates the return on investment. This requires a focus on both the anticipation of new knowledge needs and pressure on the speed of its deployment.

KM can help firms be more agile in two ways: through knowledge portfolio management and through collaborative learning facilitation

(Dove, 2003). Knowledge portfolio management can help organisations to identify, acquire, diffuse and renew all knowledge that the organisation requires. Collaborative learning supported by a purposeful infrastructure and culture can bring more diversity of thought and thus enable organisations to learn faster. Organisations knowing more and acting sooner are more likely to survive and even lead in their business environment, as demonstrated by Case study 7.4 on the Swiss travel agency Kuoni.

Case study 7.4

Kuoni

The competitive environment for the business travel sector changed dramatically in the 1990s. Providers of services specialised rapidly and the technology that they used became more complex. Many business trips were international, and there were many ways of making bookings and arrangements. This increased the pressure on those employees who were responsible for arranging a company's business travel. They often felt overwhelmed with organising it all themselves. As such, companies that seek support from travel agencies expect high levels of organisational ability and technical competence. In addition, transparency of costs has become an important factor, because of the growth in company expenditure on business trips: after salaries and IT, travel is often the third major expense category.

In view of the dynamic growth of the business travel sector, Kuoni decided to transform itself from a simple travel agency into a 'business travel information management company', which aimed to provide its customers the kind of information they need, and hence to improve their management of business travel. The strategy of focusing on offering knowledge-enriched services determined its image and great success.

Kuoni now provides knowledge-intensive services in the business travel sector. In its efforts to become the 'trustee of the travel budget', it offers customers a comprehensive range of services, including special offers and special trips to trade fairs, as well as ordinary business trips. Kuoni's computerised customer files contain all data relevant to business travel for their clients such as class of travel, car rental category and personal preferences regarding seating and food.

To adopt a knowledge-oriented approach to customer support, Kuoni has developed a unique system called 'Knows' which stands for 'Kuoni nationally offered worldwide statistics'. 'Knows' helps analyse the cost of journeys for Kuoni's customers by enabling the company to assemble and process all data on the travel which a customer had previously arranged through Kuoni. The data package can be evaluated and presented according to customer requirements, and affords maximum transparency of travel costs. Spending on flights, hotels and car rental can be broken down according to destination, class of travel, provider and period. Historical comparison for the cost incurred can also be provided. Management information flows direct to the customer from all business destinations through the network of Kuoni associates in the Business Travel International (BTI) Association.

The information, presented in a convenient format, makes it easy to answer questions like which airline has attracted the greatest share of bookings or which destination is the most expensive. 'Knows' helps the customer monitor business travel more efficiently and locate opportunities for bulk bookings which carry discounts. This value-added service helps Kuoni to attract and retain its customers in the long term.

Source: Probst et al. (2000).

KM strategies for competitiveness

The above examples illustrate selected KM outcomes and successful KM strategies that led to those outcomes. For a theoretical understanding of how KM elements are linked to organisational competitiveness, readers are referred to Holsapple and Singh's knowledge chain model (2003). The model, based on Porter's value chain model, comprises five prime activities that manipulate knowledge – acquisition, selection, generation, internalisation and externalisation – and four secondary activities that enable, support and guide their performance – leadership, coordination, control and measurement. The model proposes that each of these activities has a role in adding value to an organisation by increasing its competitiveness through improved productivity, agility, reputation and innovation. The following subsections extend this model to include three KM dimensions (knowledge enablers, knowledge processes and knowledge assets) and briefly summarise their relationships to organisational competitiveness.

Knowledge enablers and competitiveness

Based on the evidence from a large number of successful companies, the following series of propositions was put forward regarding the relationships between various socio-technical knowledge enablers and competitiveness (Holsapple and Singh, 2003).

For example, defining clear objectives and measuring results against these objectives can lead to business improvements. Valuing business customers, employees' competencies, processes and systems can lead to greater productivity, enhanced image and increased income. Productivity gains and enhanced earnings can also be achieved by exploiting employee capabilities more effectively.

Control initiatives that place knowledge in order by assessing, categorising and protecting its content can foster greater productivity in the use of knowledge. Communication structures using intranets that allow people to communicate with customers faster can improve responsiveness, and thus enhance reputation.

Coordination of activities can be done in a way that speeds up the product development process resulting in agility and innovation. Flattening hierarchical structures can improve communication channels for knowledge flows among employees and enable them to act productively. Communication technologies can further help employees to relay knowledge faster, and thus improve responsiveness to customers.

Leadership can add value to the firm by creating a vision for the future, aligning strategies, motivating and inspiring people and driving change. It can bring changes in behaviour and culture, recognise and reward desirable behaviours and enhance employees' morale, and thus productivity and creativity.

Knowledge processes and competitiveness

The Holsapple and Singh (2003) knowledge chain model suggests that various knowledge processes can be the sources of competitiveness. However, to achieve a competitive advantage, an organisation needs to be able to adopt and execute these knowledge processes better than its competitors.

For example, monitoring and rapidly acquiring the latest knowledge from external sources of expertise and their realisation in refined production processes can help organisations to achieve innovative advances. Providing reliable and authoritative content from credible external sources can also improve the effectiveness of in-house decision-making, and ensure timely transfer of knowledge to where it is needed within the organisation.

Similarly, locating, collecting, packaging and transferring knowledge from various internal sources can reduce product design and development time significantly, and thus enhance innovation and productivity. Selecting and hiring the best people can also have a positive impact on both innovation and productivity. Profiling customers can help companies make more consistent, accurate and faster decisions about customers. Discovering valuable knowledge about product flows and supply and demand patterns can help derive new services and increase shareholder return. Advanced knowledge-mining techniques can help consultants to evaluate, discover and synthetise high-quality knowledge to help their clients to be successful in their business.

Effective internalisation of standards and aspirations can be the key driver of value and reputation. Furthermore, effective internalisation of potential solutions can improve employees' problem-solving skills. Corporate knowledge maps can help better internalise the rich pool of knowledge existing within the company, and thus lead to productivity gains.

Publishing findings in leading outlets is a way of knowledge externalisation that can help organisations to build their reputation and attract top talent. 'Productising' existing knowledge, that is, selecting, organising, distilling and packaging knowledge, can result in a wider range of offerings to customers. Intelligent information systems, e.g. expert systems, can be used to assist with the effective and efficient externalisation of product expertise to customers.

Knowledge assets and competitiveness

The Handzic (2004) KM framework suggests an indirect impact of knowledge enablers and processes on competitiveness through their impact on knowledge. This framework suggests that the main role of knowledge enablers is to help organisations to create a knowledge-conducive climate, facilitate knowledge processes and provide feedback for potential adjustment of KM strategies over time. It also suggests that the main role of knowledge processes is to move or modify knowledge stocks. The assumption is that the better the processes of knowledge generation, sharing, capture and discovery, the greater the likelihood that the knowledge needed will be available, leading to more effective and innovative organisational performance. From this perspective, 'knowledge' is the central driver of competitiveness.

Improved knowledge can lead to productivity gains in a number of ways (Wiig and Jooste, 2003). For example, gains can be achieved by making it possible for people to be faster and more innovative by streamlining products and processes, and so on. To be productive people need to possess task-specific, navigational and general knowledge, as well as declarative and methodological meta-knowledge. In addition, organisations need to possess structural knowledge embedded in systems and procedures to ascertain secure, appropriate and effective handling of tasks, issues and opportunities. Enhanced personal knowledge can lead to the more effective performance of individual workers, while enhanced structural knowledge is an important contributor to improved enterprise performance.

Hansen et al. (1999) link explicit knowledge to more efficient and effective services and tacit knowledge to innovativeness and solutions to unique and high-level strategic problems. No matter what form knowledge takes, difficult to replicate or imitate knowledge assets have the greatest impact on the market share and profitability of the firm (Teece and Pisano, 2003).

Conclusion

This chapter addresses the outcomes of knowledge management and identifies successful strategies leading to these outcomes. The chapter concentrates on three main types of KM outcomes: knowledge retention, productivity improvement and innovation.

To be successful in retaining knowledge, organisations need to identify critical knowledge, use different tools to retain it, build an open, responsive and trusting environment and integrate knowledge processes with learning and innovation.

For enhancing competitive productivity, organisations need to provide better knowledge, change organisational processes and culture and employ an appropriate mix of technologies to enable access to the knowledge that people need, at the time they need it, in the form that they need it.

To be successful in innovation, organisations need to take a strategic view of knowledge, formulate knowledge visions, tear down knowledge barriers, develop new corporate values and trust, catalyse and coordinate knowledge creation, manage the various contexts involved, develop a conversational culture, globalise local knowledge and localise global knowledge.

Above all, it is important to note that these specific strategies need to be aligned with the overall organisational goals and missions.

References

Arthur Andersen (1998) *The Knowledge Management Practices Book: A guide to who's doing what in organisational knowledge management*, The Global Best Practices Research Team, Arthur Andersen, January.

Becerra-Fernandez, I., Gonzales, A. and Sabherwal, R. (2004) *Knowledge Management: Challenges, Solutions, and Technologies*. Upper Saddle River, NJ: Pearson Education.

Davenport, T.H., De Long, D.W. and Breers, M.C. (1998) 'Successful knowledge management projects', *Sloan Management Review*, Winter, 43–57.

Dove, R. (2003) 'Knowledge management and agility: relationship and roles', in C.W. Holsapple (ed.), *Handbook on Knowledge Management*, Vol. 2. Berlin: Springer, pp. 309–30.

Earl, M. (2001) 'Knowledge management strategies: toward a taxonomy', *Journal of Management Information Systems*, 18 (1): 215–33.

Frank, B. (2002) 'Five tips to reduce knowledge loss', *In Thought and Practice: Journal of the KM Professional Society*, December: 1–3.

Handzic, M. (2003) 'Empowering society through knowledge records', in M.A. Wimmer (ed.), *Proceedings of IFIP International Working Conference on Knowledge Management in Electronic Government (KMGov 2003)*, Rhodes, 26–28 May, pp. 262–7.

Handzic, M. (2004) *Knowledge Management through the Technology Glass*. Singapore: World Scientific.

Handzic, M. and Bewsell, G. (2003) 'Corporate memories: tombs or wellsprings of knowledge?', in *Proceedings of IRMA2003 Conference*, USA.

Handzic, M. and Chaimungkalanont, M. (2003) 'The impact of socialisation on organisational creativity', in *Proceedings of the European Conference on Knowledge Management (ECKM 2003)*, Oxford, 18–19 September.

Hansen, M.T., Nohria, N. and Tierney, T. (1999) 'What's your strategy for managing knowledge?', *Harvard Business Review*, 77 (2): 106–16.

Holsapple, C.W. and Singh, M. (2003) 'The knowledge chain model: activities for competitiveness', in C.W. Holsapple (ed.), *Handbook on Knowledge Management*, Vol. 2. Berlin: Springer, pp. 215–51.

Land, L.P.W., Land, M. and Handzic, M. (2002) 'Retaining organisational knowledge: a case study of an Australian construction company', *Journal of Information and Knowledge Management*, 1 (2): 119–29.

Nonaka, I. and Nishiguchi, T. (2001) *Knowledge Emergence.* New York: Oxford University Press.

O'Dell, C., Elliot, S. and Hubert, C. (2003) 'Achieving knowledge management outcomes', in C.W. Holsapple (ed.), *Handbook on Knowledge Management*, Vol. 2. Berlin: Springer, pp. 253–88.

Probst, G.J.B., Raub, S. and Romhart, K. (2000) *Managing Knowledge: Building Blocks for Success.* England: John Wiley and Sons, pp. 9–10.

Rollo, C. and Clarke, T. (2001) *International Best Practice: Case Studies in Knowledge Management.* Standards Australia Int.

Snowden, D. (2003) 'Innovation as an objective of knowledge management. Part I: The landscape of management', *Knowledge Management Research and Practice*, 1 (2): 113–19.

Teece, D.J. and Pisano, G. (2003) 'The dynamic capabilities of firms', in C.W. Holsapple (ed.), *Handbook on Knowledge Management*, Vol. 2. Berlin: Springer, pp. 195–214.

Von Krogh, G., Ichijo, K. and Nonaka, I. (2000) *Enabling Knowledge Creation.* New York: Oxford University Press.

Wiig, K.M. and Jooste, A. (2003) 'Exploiting knowledge for productivity gains', in C.W. Holsapple (ed.), *Handbook on Knowledge Management*, Vol. 2. Berlin: Springer, pp. 289–308.

8

Issues and challenges for KM practice and research

Introduction

Although KM is currently highly fashionable and visible, there is a danger that the hype surrounding KM may kill off the field as a fad. This is because KM is relatively immature, prone to misconceptions and misappropriations, and there are many unresolved issues that need to be addressed before KM evolves into a mature discipline. According to Handzic and Hasan (2003), two major challenges for KM lie in: (1) bridging the gap between theory and practice and thus providing well-established KM strategies, tools and procedures for managers; and (2) advancing understanding of KM and achieving an objective picture of the field that integrates diverse perspectives based on formal and sound research.

Those authors who have taken up the first, practice-oriented challenge have provided sets of recommended phases, guidelines and flexible integrated methodologies for conducting KM in organisations (Handzic, 2004a, 2004b; Liebowitz and Megbolugbe, 2003). These methods are directed principally at managers and KM practitioners. Typically, they identify 'proven' critical steps, key factors and possible alternative paths, and thus put into the hands of managers practical tools that support knowledge enabling in their organisations.

There is a fundamental tension in organisations between the development of knowledge and the desire for knowledge protection. Chae and Bloodgood (2004) call it the 'paradox of belonging'. This tension can also be viewed as the tension between openness and closure, or between cooperation and competition. On the one hand, the development of knowledge assets requires openness and knowledge sharing by individuals and groups, within and across organisations. On the other hand, the firm's competitive advantage is often seen as lying in its ability to prevent knowledge leaking across its potentially porous boundaries. This chapter explores these tensions and suggests a possible way of managing them.

With respect to the second, research-orientated challenge, many authors provide reviews of lessons learnt and suggest future research directions (Alavi and Leidner, 2001; Handzic and Hasan, 2003). From what we have learnt so far, KM needs to be integrated into the strategic management of the organisation. Knowledge context, process and content all need to be carefully managed in order to preserve or create value for an organisation. However, this can only be achieved by applying those KM methods, solutions and tools that are based on sound and formal research.

Some researchers argue that more rigour must be put into KM research (Handzic and Hasan, 2003) if it is to reliably inform KM practice. Therefore, this chapter also proposes a rigorous multi-method research agenda in KM processes and the socio-technical circumstances surrounding KM. It is hoped that such an agenda will help achieve the required objectivity and generality, and alleviate the scepticism surrounding the practical value of academic research.

Resolving the tension between knowledge development and knowledge protection

Authors from the knowledge development research stream (Chae and Bloodgood, 2004) claim that no business is an island, and emphasise the need for openness and knowledge sharing through partnerships and alliances. Learning from the experience of others is considered the key capability that organisations must possess. They also warn that closed organisations cannot survive over the long run and that isolation simply means death.

On the other hand, the proponents of knowledge protection emphasise that firms need to have institutional capabilities which will allow them to protect knowledge from imitation and expropriation. The most visible form of knowledge protection is afforded by intellectual property

(IP) rights worldwide. However, intellectual property protection could hamper knowledge sharing. This is because once knowledge takes the form of IP, access to that knowledge is controlled.

Recognising the fact that intellectual property rights may present a serious challenge to the growth and proliferation of knowledge assets, we explore the pros and cons of protecting knowledge assets through intellectual property rights, and provide some suggestions for organisations as to how to approach this issue. Before we commence, we will look at what we mean by intellectual property.

The concept of intellectual property

The World Intellectual Property Organisation (WIPO) defines intellectual property as rights relating to intellectual activity in the industrial, scientific, literary and artistic fields (WIPO, 2004). It refers to any product of human intellect such as an idea, invention, expression, unique name, method or industrial process. Generally, IP can be understood as the legal mechanism that provides protection of one's creative effort. This simply means that the owner of the intellectual property rights can be awarded damages if unauthorised parties try to use or infringe upon the use of the intellectual property.

Intellectual property is different from intellectual capital (Wilkins et al., 1997; Smith and Hansen, 2002). Intellectual capital includes a subset of organisational core capabilities (i.e. technical knowledge and understanding, as well as its practices, processes or methods by which those assets are deployed to create value) that have been formalised and captured. Intellectual capital is what a firm needs to innovate, grow and ensure competitive advantage. It has to have an economic value for the firm that is determined by its economic properties rather than defined by the law.

In contrast, what constitutes IP is a matter of law, and the value of the intellectual property depends on the scope of the protection afforded by the law. In general, IP rights represent a legal recognition of ownership granted by the government to the party for creative or research effort that gives the party the right to fully exploit (e.g. own, sell, license or bequeath) IP. Usually, only a small portion of organisational intellectual capital gets such legal protection as shown in Figure 8.1.

It is also important to remember that the extent of protection varies from country to country. The lack of international harmonisation of IP

Figure 8.1 Intellectual property, intellectual capital and core capability

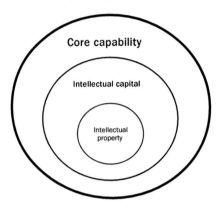

laws makes it easy for multinationals to arbitrage across nations and exploit weaknesses in national IP systems. In addition, the scope of IP categories may change over time due to new socio-technical developments (McKeough et al., 2004). In the light of this, there have been attempts by the World Trade Organisation (WTO) to foster global integration of IP laws (Lang, 2001).

Types of IP protection

The nature of the intellectual property determines the type of protection needed. Legal rights of IP ownership are either granted automatically upon the creation of the work or require formal steps to register and obtain them. IP that requires formal registration includes: patents (e.g. black box flight recorder), trademarks (e.g. Mambo, a famous Australian designer label), designs (e.g. the pattern of Dunlop tyre treads) and plant breeders' rights (e.g. a new variety of plant). Forms of IP that do not require formal registration include: copyright (e.g. a journal article, novel, cartoon or recorded musical work), circuit layout rights (e.g. 3D computer chips) and trade secrets (e.g. the formula for Coca-Cola). More detailed descriptions of the different types of IP are provided in the box below (IP Australia, 2004).

The choice of the type of protection is important for directing the use and development of IP or for granting others permission to do so. Priority and timing are also of critical importance for IP protection. Starting the IP strategy early can help protect an idea or work from the initial stages. Relevant documentation, such as a lab book, may be important evidence in any eventual dispute.

Types of intellectual property

Patents
According to the World Intellectual Property Organisation (WIPO), a patent is an exclusive right granted for an invention. It deems an invention to be a new product or a process that provides a new way of doing something or offers a new approach to a problem. A patent generally provides protection for the invention to the owner of the patent for a limited period of 20 years.

Trademarks
A trademark is a distinctive sign that provides a unique identification to certain goods or services produced or provided by a specific person or enterprise. Once a trademark is registered, it offers the owner of the mark the exclusive legal right to use, license and sell the mark. A trademark can have an infinite life, provided the owner keeps the registration current. The interval period for a renewal of registration may vary among nations. Domain names (Internet addresses) can also be registered as trademarks, provided that they meet the requirements of the relevant acts.

Designs
Registered designs are used to protect the visual appearance of a manufactured good. Registration gives the owner a legally enforceable right to use the product design to gain a competitive edge and prevent others from using the design without agreement. The period of protection is initially for 12 months, but it can be extended for up to 16 years.

Plant breeders' rights
This classification is used to protect new varieties of plants by giving exclusive commercial rights to owners to market a new variety of plant or its reproductive material. These rights do not extend to the use of the variety in plant breeding or retention of seed for the production of another crop on their land. The rights are valid for up to 25 years for trees and vines and 20 years for other species.

Copyrights
Copyright is an exclusive legal right automatically given to creators for their literary and artistic works. The owner of the copyright for a work holds the exclusive right to use or authorise others to use the work. According to the relevant WIPO treaties, copyright allows the owner of a

---

copyright to obtain financial benefits from selling the right, generally for a limited period of 50 years after the death of the creator.

Circuit layout rights

These rights automatically protect original layout designs for integrated circuits and computer chips. Although based on copyright law principles, they are a separate and unique form of protection. Circuit layout rights allow the owner to copy the layout, make circuits from the layout and exploit it commercially for a period of 20 years.

Trade secrets

This classification provides effective protection for some technologies and know-how-type knowledge. Ideally, trade secrets are backed up by signing a confidentiality agreement with every person who has knowledge of the secret. Secrecy, however, does not stop anyone else from inventing the same product or process independently and exploiting it commercially. Artistic creations, mathematical methods, plans, schemes or other purely mental processes cannot be patented.

Source: IP Australia (2004).

In addition to legal protection, there are many other types of technological and managerial control systems that a firm can establish to protect its intellectual assets (Jamieson and Handzic, 2003). In a sophisticated IT system, knowledge can be protected by filename, username or password that will determine what rights the user has. Screen and keystroke monitoring systems and firewalls can be used to protect knowledge from hackers or industrial espionage. With respect to managerial controls, a firm can establish rules of conduct to cover issues such as exclusivity protocols, confidentiality and non-disclosure of location of work. Job design into disaggregated tasks and deferred incentive plans may help keep knowledge inside the firm.

Protection pros and cons

The pressure for the expansion of intellectual property protection over knowledge assets has brought corresponding debates and issues as to whether such expansion is good or bad for the economy and society as a whole (David and Foray, 2002).

Some inventors are not concerned with the fact that their ideas are being used by others. For example, many authors are happy with the emerging 'right to copy' rule (Raich, 2000), which gives everybody the right to copy parts of their text, on the condition that they quote the source. In this way, these authors feel that their efforts have been justified and recognised. Such behaviour is not limited to individuals; it also extends to many institutions.

However, there are still many parties who feel that they need to prevent others from reaping the fruits of their effort. There are many documented examples of good ideas that are picked up by other companies or individuals, who go on to make enormous profits from their sale without any need to pay royalties or make acknowledgement of contribution to the originators.

The case of Frank Bannigan, managing director of Kambrook, is a good example of the pitfalls that arise from not adequately protecting your IP. In 1972, Mr Bannigan developed the electrical power-board. The product was a huge success and was the basis for Kambrook's growth to become a major producer of electrical appliances. Kambrook could have enjoyed a 20-year monopoly over the power-board market. However, the power-board was not patented and Kambrook ended up sharing the market with many other manufacturers. According to Mr Bannigan, Kambrook has probably lost millions of dollars in royalties alone. This haunts the inventor whenever he goes into a department store and sees the wide range of power-boards on offer. Today, Kambrook has a number of patents and pending applications for improvements in a range of consumer goods (IP Australia, 2004).

The above examples indicate the existence of moral and economic dilemmas that arise as a result of IP. Therefore, an important part of an organisation's strategy for IP will need to take into account the tension between fostering the growth of knowledge assets through KM techniques such as sharing and IP regimes that prevent their free flow. In the attempt to resolve this tension, we will first analyse the various arguments that are against or in favour of IP rights.

Arguments against IP

- *IP creates a monopoly over knowledge exploitation.* Some researchers argue that IP rights have a negative long-term effect for economic growth, as they create a monopoly over the commercial exploitation of knowledge (David, 2004). They warn that the lack of competition leads to inefficient allocation of resources and hinders the effective access to and use of knowledge.

- *IP decreases the availability of knowledge in the public domain.* There is a widespread recognition that knowledge is different from other goods in that it can be reused without being depleted. Thus some researchers argue that it should not be afforded protection like other goods, but be part of the public domain (David and Foray, 2002). According to these researchers, increasing protection decreases the availability of knowledge in the public domain, and thus has a negative effect on the intellectual richness of people's lives. Copyleft advocacy networks also perceive IP protection as an obstruction to the greater interests of organisations and the public domain (Carayannis and Alexander 1999).

Copyleft is a form of an IP agreement that is applied to a creative product as it is published. Copyleft permits all subsequent users to reproduce, modify or adapt the original creation as they require, thus developing new and different creations. The primary condition of the Copyleft agreement is that any new creation based on the original work must also be covered by the same copyleft agreement, thereby permitting the continuing development of new creative products.

Source: Pike (2002).

- *IP limits creativity and innovation.* Knowledge is seen as both an input and an output of KM process. IP limits and prescribes the use of the output by assigning IP rights to various creations and innovations. This, in turn, restricts the input for future creations and innovations (Wagner, 2003). Researchers warn that this may be detrimental to productivity in the knowledge economy and the long-term vitality of science.

- *IP does not provide full protection.* Some researchers argue against IP on the basis that it does not offer full protection for knowledge assets. For example, patents can be challenged and even overturned. Copyrights are costly to enforce and trade secrets laws apply only to codified knowledge in continuous use. Non-continuous knowledge such as contract bids, plans or prototypes as well as tacit knowledge are not protected. Anton and Yao (2004) identify a major weakness of the IP regime in that innovators need to disclose valuable knowledge to the public. As a result, protection might cause a loss of firm value

(Schrader, 1991). Due to the risks associated with unauthorised imitation, many firms keep their innovations secret. This limits the knowledge-rich environment necessary for productivity in a knowledge-based economy.

- *IP increases costs and is difficult to value.* Even if it would be possible to protect knowledge assets with IP rights in an appropriate way, the cost of doing so would be high. The large amount of time and money needed to be invested in the bureaucratic process makes the economic argument for protection questionable. Moreover, some researchers warn that intellectual assets need not necessarily have any economic value to be eligible for protection (Wilkins et al., 1997). This further makes valuing of IP problematic.

Arguments in favour of IP

- *IP is a source of revenue.* The most important argument in favour of IP rights is the possibility of deriving income from one's creative effort. For example, licencing revenues accounted for a fifth of IBM's profit in 1999. IP is also suitable as security for debt finance (Bezant, 1998). As we become increasingly familiar with a post-capitalist knowledge-based economy, new opportunities for the application of IP are likely to arise. In general, the costs of creating something new are quite high, and if the creators have no rights to derive an income from their work they may cease to create or create less (David, 2004). Thus IP represents an important incentive to creators for continuous innovation because they can be assured that they will reap the benefits.

- *IP increases availability of knowledge in the public domain.* Some researchers challenge the idea that IP rights diminish the amount of knowledge in the public domain (Wagner, 2003). Instead, they argue the fact that IP increases rather than decreases the availability of public knowledge. One reason given is that knowledge cannot be perfectly controlled because it cannot all be captured. The indirect knowledge around IP will provide a platform through which knowledge can be built upon and proliferate.

- *IP decreases knowledge hoarding.* Some researchers argue that one of the reasons why a company should protect its IP is that, by so doing, they can actually help to decrease the tendency to hoard knowledge

(Gilmour, 2003). They warn that most of the time a company's knowledge-sharing model wrongly assumes that people are willing to share their most valuable knowledge without getting any benefit from it. However, distributing ideas without any protection could be harmful to the originator if others can claim these as their own ideas without consequences. Consequently, creative effort spent in developing these ideas could result in loss. Once the individual can be sure that their efforts spent in developing new ideas will be acknowledged and rewarded, their willingness to share and distribute those ideas would increase.

- *IP resolves ethical issues.* The underlying rationale for IP is partly based on ethical considerations. It is assumed that people have a natural right to claim benefits that arise from the property created in their minds (McKeough et al., 2004). In addition to the right to be identified with their creation, they also have control over how that creation is reproduced or used by others. It is considered unfair for others to reap the benefits of work created by another. However, as long as there is no protection in place, some people will be always willing to steal ideas from others and claim them as their own. Adding to this problem is the increased possibility for easy copying and stealing of digital content that comes along with the rapid development of IT. According to Laudon and Laudon (2004), routine thefts threaten to reduce the speed of introducing new knowledge and therefore threaten further advances in productivity. IP rights address this threat through punitive measures for infringements.

Dialectic approach to KM

Based on the above overview, it can be argued that a balance needs to be found within the social, political and legal structures to take into account the various benefits and costs of IP rights for knowledge assets in the new knowledge-based economy. According to Teece (2000), organisations need: to take into account that different entities require different degrees of openness and closure; to recognise the importance of ownership protection, as well as keeping the channels open for the free flow of knowledge; to recognise the fuzziness of IP boundaries and the ethical issues involved in determining who exactly owns the knowledge; and to recognise the limitations and costs associated with IP protection.

A dialectic perspective on KM proposed by Chae and Bloodgood (2004) recognises that both closure and openness, competition and cooperation coexist in organisations. They argue that effective KM strategy needs to focus simultaneously on both. Their recent work suggests that transactional and relational strategies reinforce each other. Transactional strategies draw on monopolistic competition and focus on short-term profit maximisation, while relational strategies emphasise long-term mutually beneficial relationships between the organisation and industrial networks, and interaction to develop and build these relationships. They suggest that neither too much nor too little of these opposites is desirable for successful KM. Thus they argue the fact that a successful strategy must emphasise long-term relationships and short-term transactions, and see negotiation as being both competitive and cooperative rather than one or the other.

They suggest that a major challenge for KM is to enable and support the emergence of dialectic belonging. They identify several organisational characteristics that can facilitate this. Communities of practice assist with creating the right conditions for intra-organisational learning and networks of practice (NoP) for inter-organisational learning. A new mindset on the organisational boundary is proposed that sees competitors more as a means of learning than as a hostile threat, since they both are part of an interrelated business ecosystem. Firms that feed into the ecology also feed off it, and thus coevolve their capabilities. Distributed gatekeeping and extended grafting of external knowledge are two specific mechanisms believed to facilitate exploration. Gatekeepers enable organisational expertise to be moved to the front line, while grafting speeds up the exploration through external sourcing. In summary, these guidelines offer some answers on how to strike the right balance that may help organisations to better plan their competitive strategies.

Putting rigour into KM research

We have presented a comprehensive discussion of several important topics in KM including KM foundations, drivers, elements and outcomes drawing from a broad range of research in the KM literature. KM is an emerging phenomenon and is still evolving. Much more research is needed so that knowledge about how knowledge is developed can be accumulated and understanding about KM can be advanced.

In the remainder of this chapter, we briefly summarise what we have learned to date and then present a research agenda that aims to help move the discipline forward.

KM foundations

The overview of existing conceptual developments in knowledge management presented in Chapter 1 indicates that the field is evolving towards greater integration and more holistic approaches. Following the current tacit–explicit knowledge conversion (SECI) model and the earlier business process re-engineering (BPR) initiatives, Snowden (2002) suggests that we are now entering the 'third generation of knowledge management' which embraces the paradoxical nature of knowledge as both a thing and a flow, and looks for knowledge in new and different ways.

KM drivers

KM needs to be integrated into an organisation's strategic management. Our analysis in Chapter 2 reveals that corporate strategies differ in their focus on existing or new knowledge (Von Krogh et al., 2000). Survival strategies concentrate on KM initiatives around capturing and locating valuable company knowledge and making the maximum use of existing knowledge in order to minimise risk and improve efficiency. Advancement strategies on the other hand focus on a new generation of knowledge and processes necessary for enabling successful innovation.

KM elements

One of the key propositions of this book is that the context, process and content aspects of knowledge are all important elements for KM and need to be managed. The key learning that emerges from Chapters 3–6 is that the effectiveness of a knowledge process depends on the particular context in which knowledge is being generated, transferred and applied, and that the choice of the most appropriate process to deliver knowledge content is highly contingent upon the nature of that content.

Bureaucratic context is good as a training environment, communities of practice encourage sharing, informal contexts provide shared understanding through stories and symbols, and innovative contexts require action and risk-taking to impose order on chaos (Snowden, 2002). Furthermore, cataloguing and describing legitimate best practices is the best way to convey what is known. With respect to the knowable, organisations need to learn from history which components and relationships are important and use them to create predictive and prescriptive models. Exploring emerging patterns is the key to managing complexity, while the only way to learn in the realm of chaos is to create new patterns and break down the old ones.

KM outcomes

KM produces true added value only when knowledge is applied to marketable products and services. Knowledge applications can take many different forms. Chapter 7 of this book illustrated some innovative arenas where such knowledge application takes place. In summary, what we have learned and presented in this book provides a valuable source of ideas for practical knowledge management, and directions for developing a future research agenda.

Research agenda for KM

Given the multidisciplinary nature of KM, it is not surprising that there is a variety of themes, topics and methods proposed for KM research.

The Knowledge Management Research Group (KMRG),[1] specialising in socio-technical enablers and processes of knowledge development, identifies the following four broad themes for KM research:

- knowledge storage and organisation;
- knowledge discovery and visualisation;
- knowledge sharing through socialisation; and
- creativity and knowledge generation.

The following sections present specific research issues and directions with respect to each individual theme. For further information see also Handzic and Hasan (2003).

Knowledge storage and organisation

Theoretically, the availability of explicit contextual knowledge can play an important role in improving employees' knowledge work. However, processing increased amounts of artefacts is a cognitive task that induces higher demands on the mental resources of the person and increases the complexity of the problem. This in turn may negatively affect the nature of knowledge acquisition, utilisation and performance. With modern technology generating a growing abundance of knowledge artefacts, it is of particular interest to examine whether and how their availability in computerised repositories may affect individual employees' working knowledge, and what impact this may have on the quality of their subsequent performance.

In summary, research is needed to address the following questions regarding knowledge capture, storage and organisation:

- What conditions are effective in encouraging knowledge contributions to knowledge stores?

- What knowledge and context should be included in repositories?

- How is stored knowledge utilised?

Knowledge discovery and visualisation

The growing number of electronic transactions among organisations and their customers generates large volumes of electronic data that are becoming an increasingly important new source of organisational knowledge. Vast amounts of data accumulated in organisational databases may contain potentially valuable new knowledge. Hence, one of the main KM issues is concerned with the discovery of knowledge that is 'hidden' in these electronic transactions, and the utilisation of the extracted knowledge to support business tasks.

Some important research questions regarding knowledge discovery and visualisation are:

- What conditions are effective in encouraging knowledge discovery?

- What retrieval mechanisms are most effective in enabling knowledge discovery?

- What visual presentation forms enhance understanding?

Socialisation and knowledge sharing

Some authors suggest that new knowledge always begins with the individual, but that making personal knowledge available to others is the central activity of the knowledge-creating company (Nonaka and Takeuchi, 1995). The spiral knowledge model assumes that the process of sharing will result in the organisational amplification and exponential growth of working knowledge. However, given the current infancy of knowledge management research, there is little empirical evidence regarding the ways in which tacit knowledge is actually acquired and shared, and the impact it has on performance.

Future research could address these questions:

- How can knowledge be effectively shared among individuals or groups?

- What organisational and technical strategies are effective in facilitating knowledge sharing?

- What social, cultural or technical attributes of organisational settings encourage knowledge sharing?

Creativity and knowledge generation

Innovation is at the heart of the new economy. There is a widespread recognition in the knowledge management literature of the critical importance of creativity and innovation for organisational success in the changing environment. Some theorists believe that creativity is reserved only for the gifted. Others see creativity as a skill that can be learned (Ford, 1996). Therefore, future research may address the issue, by exploring theories, practices and technological solutions that may stimulate creative and innovative thinking. New ways of conducting business also requires people with multidisciplinary knowledge and skills. Education needs to develop new curricula and find more effective ways to transfer expert professional knowledge to junior and young professionals. Future research may look at new instructional techniques and advanced technologies to support accelerated and more effective learning.

The main research questions concerning creativity and knowledge generation are:

- What conditions foster new knowledge creation?
- What cultures and technologies are enablers and facilitators of knowledge creation processes?
- How is new knowledge evaluated and adopted?

Research methods

There is a widespread recognition in the KM community of the importance of suitable research methods for the field. Despite this, the question of which research methods are most appropriate for KM research still remains unanswered. This is partly because the KM discipline draws upon diverse fields and disciplines that encompass different research traditions. There are also a lot of tensions and misunderstandings between proponents of different paradigms.

The literature considers three broad research paradigms: positivist, interpretivist and critical. Each of these paradigms reflects a basic set of philosophical beliefs about the nature of the world and provides guidelines and principles concerning the way research is conducted (Cavana et al., 2001). Positivist research uses deductive reasoning, beginning with a theoretical position and moving towards concrete empirical evidence to identify a set of universal laws. Interpretivist research assumes that the reality is socially constructed and is interested in understanding people's perceptions. Critical research is action oriented towards change and interested in empowering people to create a better world for themselves.

Proponents of all three paradigms are found in KM research, as are their critics. Advocates of the positivist approach justify their following of the laboratory experiments in terms of its superiority over other methods for hypotheses testing and in determining causal relationships among factors of interest. Those in favour of the interpretivist research approach emphasise the need to collect, organise, summarise and display rich data, usually qualitative in nature, displayed according to the interpretations of the researcher(s), using their skills and expertise in the field. It is argued that all research involves some interpretation on the part of the researcher and that their background and biases should always be made explicit, and accounted for, in order for readers to better understand their findings.

Action researchers often question the usefulness of paradigm labels such as positivist, interpretivist and critical, and are interested in how different modes of enquiry contribute to 'design theory' which is needed in an applied discipline such as KM. In particular, they look at research approaches which are variously labelled as software-engineering-type research, a constructive type of research, prototyping or a systems development approach.

Some KM researchers have started to focus their research effort on multiple methods. Many researchers argue that the use of a diverse set of research methods within KM is a strength of the discipline. Different research methods may complement each other and focus on different aspects of a research problem, leading to a richer understanding of the research domain. Mingers (2001) calls this methodological pluralism. Research methods should be selected within a research programme based on their suitability for answering particular research questions.

The KMRG group attempts to provide a reconciliatory view by advocating and illustrating a multi-methodology approach and its feasibility in theory and practice. Through rigorous multi-method research such as that described in this chapter, both objectivity and generality in KM can be achieved. In particular, objectivity can be accomplished through a range of controlled studies which can reliably establish what works and what doesn't, and under what circumstances. Once a substantial collection of such studies have been accumulated, general concepts can be identified leading to integrated frameworks and models that can then be tested leading to proven practical applications.

Conclusion

The final chapter of this book, as is appropriate, examines major issues and challenges facing KM practice and research and suggests possible ways forward. With respect to practice, the main challenge is to enable and support the emergence of dialectic belonging. The chapter addresses the existing tension between knowledge development and protection and provides some tentative suggestions to organisations as to how they can approach the issue of intellectual property in a knowledge environment.

With respect to research, the challenge is to reliably inform KM practice. From what we have learnt so far, to get the most from their KM initiatives, organisations need to integrate KM into their overall strategic management processes. They also need to carefully manage knowledge content, process and context in order to preserve or create value. To further advance understanding of KM and how knowledge should be managed, much more work needs to be done. Accordingly, this chapter and the book ends with a rigorous multi-method research agenda proposed to help achieve objectivity and generality and alleviate the scepticism surrounding the practical value of academic research in KM.

Note

1. The KMRG group was established by Handzic in 2000 within the School of Information Systems, Technology and Management, UNSW, to serve as a source of expertise in KM internationally (KMRG, 2000). Its mission is to provide a broad research programme in KM, to foster collaborative work in the study of KM with business and government organisations, and to provide consulting services on best practices in KM. (More information about the group's activities can be obtained from their website on *http://www .kmrg.unsw.edu.au.*)

References

Alavi, M. and Leidner, D.E. (2001) 'Knowledge management and knowledge management systems: conceptual foundations and research issues', *MIS Quarterly*, 25 (1): 107–36.

Anton, J.J. and Yao, D.A. (2004) 'Little patents and big secrets: managing intellectual property', *Rand Journal of Economics*, 35 (1): 1–22.

Bezant, M. (1998) 'The use of intellectual property as security for debt finance', *Journal of Knowledge Management*, 1 (3): 237–62.

Carayannis, E.G. and Alexander, J. (1999) 'The wealth of knowledge: converting intellectual property to intellectual capital in a co-opetitive research and technology management setting', *International Journal of Technology Management*, 18 (3/4): 326–52.

Cavana, R.Y., Delahaye, B.L. and Sekaran, U. (2001) *Applied Business Research: Qualitative and Quantitative Methods*. Melbourne: John Wiley & Sons Australia.

Chae, B. and Bloodgood, J.M. (2004) 'Paradoxes in knowledge management: a dialectic perspective', in *Proceedings of the Tenth Americas Conference on Information Systems*. New York, August, pp. 2284–94.

David, P.A. (2004) *Can Open Science Be Protected from the Evolving Regime of IPR Protections?* Available at: *http://www.kmnetwork .com/BMA.html* (accessed 20 September 2004).

David, P.A. and Foray, D. (2002) 'An introduction to the economy of the knowledge society', *International Social Science Journal*, 54 (1): 9–23.

Ford, C.M. (1996) 'Theory of individual creative action in multiple social domains', *Academy of Management Review*, 21 (4): 1112–42.

Gilmour, D. (2003) 'How to fix knowledge management', *Harvard Business Review*, 81 (10).

Handzic, M. (2004a) 'Knowledge management in SMEs: practical guidelines', *Asia Pacific Tech Monitor*, January–February: 29–34.

Handzic, M. (2004b) 'A method for conducting knowledge management: concepts and cases', in *Proceedings of the KMChallenge 2004 Conference*, Sydney, Australia, 30–31 March.

Handzic, M. and Hasan, H. (2003) 'Continuing the knowledge management journey', in H. Hasan and M. Handzic (eds), *Australian Studies in Knowledge Management*. Wollongong: UOW Press.

IP Australia (2004) *Intellectual Property Australia*. Available at: *http://www.IPAustralia.gov.au* (accessed 20 September 2004).

Jamieson, R. and Handzic, M. (2003) 'Impact of managerial controls on the conduct of KM in organisations', in C.W. Holsapple (ed.), *Handbook on Knowledge Management*. Berlin: Springer, pp. 477–505.

KMRG (2000) *KM Research Group Annual Report 2000*. Available at: *http://www.kmrg.unsw.edu.au/kmRgAnnualReport2000.htm* (accessed 1 November 2004).

Lang, J.C. (2001) 'Management of intellectual property rights – strategic patenting', *Journal of Intellectual Capital*, 2 (1): 8–26.

Laudon, K.C. and Laudon, J.P. (2004) *Management Information Systems*, 8th edn. Upper Saddle River, NJ: Pearson Education.

Liebowitz, J. and Megbolugbe, I. (2003) 'A set of frameworks to aid the project manager in conceptualising and implementing knowledge management initiatives', *International Journal of Project Management*, 21: 189–98.

McKeough, J., Stewart, A. and Griffith, P. (2004) *Intellectual Property in Australia*, 3rd edn. Chatswood, Australia: LexisNexis Buttworths.

Mingers, J. (2001) 'Combining IS research methods: towards a pluralist methodology', *Information Systems Research*, 12 (3): 240–59.

Nonaka, I. and Takeuchi, H. (1995) *The Knowledge Creating Company: How Japanese Companies Create the Dynamics of Innovation*. New York: Oxford University Press.

Pike, G.H. (2002) 'What is right about a Copyleft?', *Information Today Magazine*, 19 (4).

Raich, M. (2000) *Managing in the Knowledge Based Economy*. Zurich, Switzerland: Raich Ltd.

Schrader, S. (1991) 'Informal technology transfer between firms: cooperation through information trading', *Research Policy*, 20: 153–70.

Smith, M. and Hansen, F. (2002) 'Managing intellectual property: a strategic point of view', *Journal of Intellectual Capital*, 3 (4): 366–74.

Snowden, D. (2002) 'Complex acts of knowing: paradox and descriptive self-awareness', in *Proceedings of the European Conference on Knowledge Management (ECKM 2002)*, Dublin, September.

Teece, D.J. (2000) 'Strategies for managing knowledge assets: the role of firm structure and industrial context', *Long Range Planning*, 33 (1): 35–54.

Von Krogh, G., Ichijo, K. and Nonaka, I. (2000) *Enabling Knowledge Creation*. New York: Oxford University Press Inc.

Wagner, R.P. (2003) 'Information wants to be free: IP and the mythologies of control', *Columbia Law Review*, 103 (40): 995–1034.

Wilkins, J., Van Wegen, B. and de Hoog, R. (1997) 'Understanding and valuing knowledge assets: overview and method', *Expert Systems with Applications*, 13 (1): 55–72.

WIPO (2004) *World Intellectual Property Organisation*. Available at: *http://www.wipo.int/* (accessed 20 September 2004).

Index

Printed in the United States
85382LV00005B/1/A